BRITISH BATTALION

XV

INTERNATIONAL BRIGADE

BRITISH BATTALION
XV
INTERNATIONAL BRIGADE

Man's dearest possession is life. And since it is granted to him to live but once, he must so live as to feel no torturing regrets for years without purpose; so live as not to be seared by the shame of a cowardly and trivial past; so live that, dying, he can say: "All my life and all my strength were given to the finest cause in the world—the fight for the liberation of mankind."

The Naval & Military Press Ltd

Published by

The Naval & Military Press Ltd
Unit 5 Riverside, Brambleside
Bellbrook Industrial Estate
Uckfield, East Sussex
TN22 1QQ England

Tel: +44 (0)1825 749494

www.naval-military-press.com
www.nmarchive.com

In reprinting in facsimile from the original, any imperfections are inevitably reproduced and the quality may fall short of modern type and cartographic standards.

"We pledge our victory as vengeance for our
We pledge to fight and carry on until Fe

rades
been destroyed throughout all the world!"

They came from Britain's towns . . .

and from Britain's countryside . . .

From the factory and the workshop and the mine—from the core of Industrial Britain—from the living heart of her people they came.

From the arts and sciences too they came—cutting short many a brilliant scholastic career—leaving behind them many a comfortable home.

OUT OF THE PROUD traditions of Britain's past they came. Part of the long struggle for freedom, carried forward from Wat Tyler through men like Byron and movements like the Chartists, through Keir Hardie to the present day. Our modern bearers of Britain's great traditions came forward in answer to the call, ready to give their lives that freedom might live.

The engraving opposite shows the great Trades Union Rally in Parliament Hill Fields, April 21, 1834, to protest against the savage sentences on the Dorchester Labourers, pioneers of Trades Union struggle in Britain. One of the moments in our history leading up to the magnificent heroism of the British Battalion.

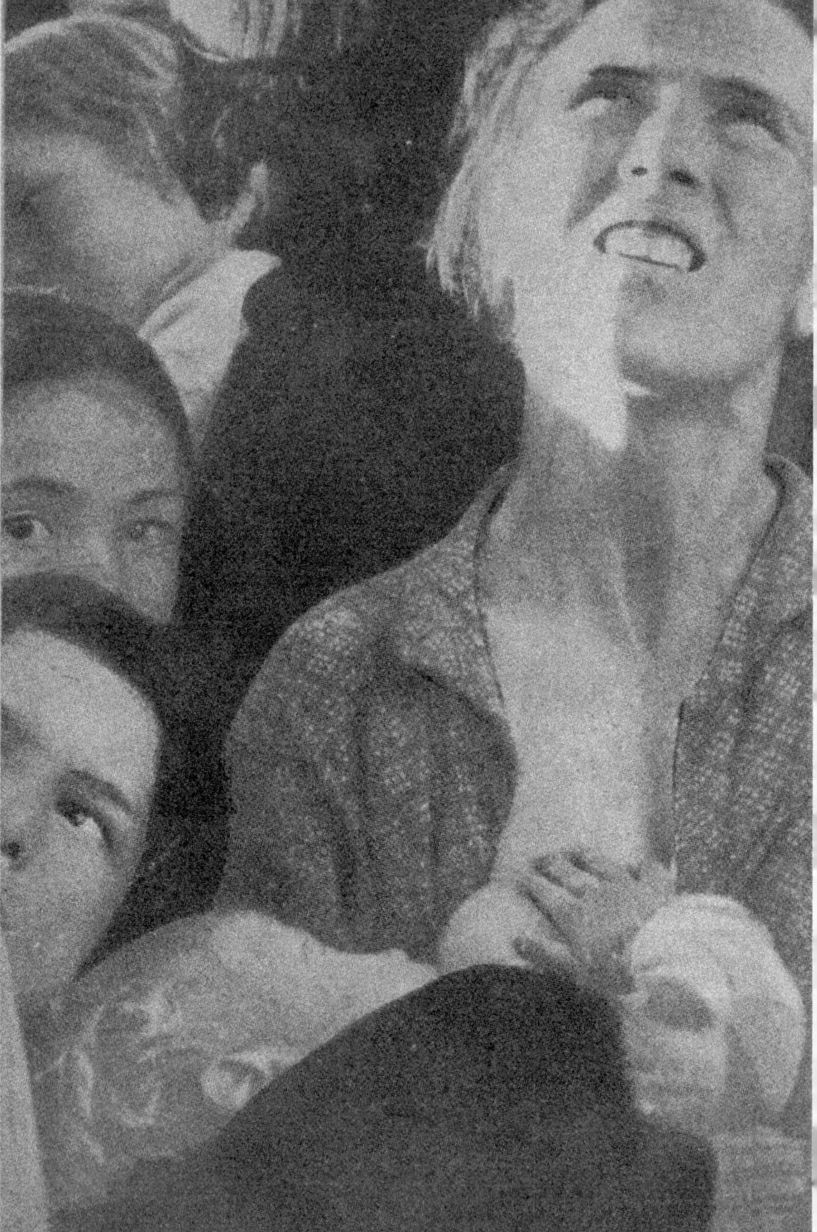

TO DEFEND LIBERTY — they typified the real Briton's hatred of the tyrant. They went to safeguard peace and the arts of peace, that humanity might go forward. They went to help the defenceless Spanish people fight the invading armies. They went to save their loved ones, and us, from the horrors of fascism. Because they loved peace, they went out to fight . . .

Britons took up Arms

" The Volunteer for Liberty," members of the International Brigade called the newspaper they produced in half a dozen languages. It was a good title.

More than 2,000 volunteers for liberty went from Britain to fight for all the things that the best of British men and women have held dear through the centuries of their history.

Those 2,000 men fought under a hot Spanish sun in a country strange to them for the same fundamental principles as John Ball and Wat Tyler fought more than five centuries earlier. Nearly five hundred of them have died. They died for reasons that are written imperishably in the traditions of their fathers and their grandfathers.

Fifteen hundred of the 2,000 were wounded; some were incapacitated for life. They limp about Britain to-day in the footsteps of John Wyclif and Jack Cade, the Chartists who followed in later years, and all those other men who have built up the story of Britain's long fight for freedom.

It was Pasionaria who when the attack on the Spanish people began cried proudly: " We would rather die on our feet than live on our knees."

That defiant sentence found an echo in the hearts of men in fifty-two lands. So the greatest epic of the 20th century began with the journey of volunteers for liberty from the countries of the world.

The came from all they corners of Europe. They rode under trains across half a dozen international boundaries. From Greece and Bulgaria and Jugoslavia and Hungary where liberty had always been difficult to hold, they made their way to Spain. They smuggled themselves out of Fascist Italy and Nazi Germany. Some of them had escaped from dictatorship to a hardly won peace in democratic countries; now they threw their peace away.

From every part of France they came; from Switzerland, Belgium and Holland, tramping along the European roads. Later they began to arrive from America, Canada, South Africa, far away Australia, often working their passage on merchant steamers.

And they came from Britain. From the Clydeside and industrial areas of Scotland where the spirit of independence has always been proud and strong; from South Wales, whose hills and valleys are haunted by memories of freedom's fight, from the North of England, where the ground is thick with traditions of a people obstinate and stiff-necked in their defiance of tyrants; from London, which has seen so many struggles for democracy.

Andre Marty, organiser of the International Brigade, wrote in a farewell message, when it was decided to withdraw the Brigade from Spain:

"The volunteers of the International Brigade have come from all classes, all political parties and trade union organisations of the world.

" Workers and farmers, artizans and tradesmen, professional men and intellectuals fought side by side in Spain, united by their desire to combat fascism. Here fought Ralph Fox, the celebrated English author, who died at his post as company commander at Andujar; here fought Lukacs, the great Hungarian author, who died fighting as a Brigade Commander at Huesca; here died the famous French surgeon, Dubois, also at his post, and thousands of others.

" You could find in the ranks of the International Brigade former officers of every army in the world. But the great majority of the International Brigade was formed of men of the working class of all countries, of old and young anti-fascist fighters.

" Here fought the German veteran Hans Beimler after his escape from a concentration camp, shoulder to shoulder with the young French worker, Bruyeres, and both of them died at their posts, comrades-in-arms against the common foe, fascism.

" Germans and Frenchmen, who 20 years ago fought against each other at Verdun, have here fought together as brothers for the first time in history—united by the same ideals, for freedom and democracy, threatened the world over by fascism."

Among the first of the volunteers from all those nations were London men. In July, 1936, when the signal for attack was made by Franco and his friends, Nat Cohen, of Whitechapel, and Sam Masters were making their way across France to Spain on a cycling holiday. Hearing the news they went on—only more quickly.

In a Barcelona barracks the two men met Felicia Brown, London artist, who had been sketching in Spain when the attack on the Republican Government began. Felicia Brown, like many Spanish women in those urgent times, took up a rifle and fought. A Fascist bullet killed her while she was going to the rescue of a wounded comrade; she was the first known British casualty. She never saw the International Brigade, but it would have delighted her heart.

Cohen and Masters found the Government forces badly in need of officers. Masters was sent to the Aragon front. Nat Cohen, who spoke Spanish, was put in charge of a company which was to help in the occupation of the island of Majorca. The Government troops landed at Majorca, but later withdrew and returned to the mainland where their help was needed.

When the Majorca expedition returned in August there was a little group of about a dozen men from Britain in Barcelona. They decided to form a British company under command of Nat Cohen, and call it after Tom Mann, the veteran British labour leader.

That little company was the forerunner of the British Battalion, and indeed of the International Brigade. The Germans formed a Thaelmann Group; the French and the Italians organised companies, too. Later they were all to merge into an " International Centuria " before the organisation of the International Brigade.

The Tom Mann Centuria had its baptism of fire on the Aragon front in October during the first night attack made by the Government forces in that area.

Meanwhile, however, Franco's threat to Madrid had grown more menacing. The international volunteers were passing through Barcelona and making direct for the Madrid front. The men from Britain came singly at first, making their way as best they could, taking week-end excursion tickets to Paris, and getting transport from there, or hitch-hiking.

The ones and twos grew into fours and fives; into bigger groups. People in the towns and villages between the border and Barcelona, between Barcelona and Madrid began to know them. Old fighting tunes of the Great War, brought on the lips of men who had now come to fight in a war that was really theirs, began to be heard in some of those villages.

The earliest British arrivals went to Albacete and

Madrigueras, where they formed the famous No. 1 Company —a company which set a high and heroic standard for the many British volunteers who followed.

The company trained intensively and with a fierce haste that made the pitiful lack of equipment then available all the more galling. Even this training was suddenly interrupted. On Christmas Eve, 1936, there came an urgent call. Reinforcements were needed on the Cordova front; the situation was critical.

Led by Captain George Nathan, an ex-British Army officer, as commander, and Ralph Fox, the distinguished writer, as political commissar, the British volunteers were rushed into action by train. Short of weapons and ammunitions, like the rest of the Republican Army, they fought with gallantry and stubbornness around Cordova and Lopera. It was in those early engagements that No. 1 Company made a name for British volunteers that was never lost.

Nathan's coolness and courage became a byword with the men. Completely fearless, he literally inspired his company, while the mature political experience of Ralph Fox completed a great leadership. The company suffered a heavy loss when first Fox and—much later—Nathan were killed.

Later the company was transferred to the Madrid front and again went into action. Then back to Madrigueras to receive a tremendous reception from the many fresh British volunteers and the inhabitants of the village.

All the world now knows the story of Spain's first spontaneous resistance to the rising organised by the Army officers and their Fascist supporters. The tale of how the people crushed by sheer mass resistance the most menacing attacks in Madrid, Barcelona and other large towns, and then turned to fight almost without arms first the Moors and well equipped army forces and later the Italians and the Germans, is a tale that will never die.

That first people's "army in overalls" went into action with the most motley collection of weapons that was ever seen. Ancient rifles, antiquated revolvers, long disused sporting guns, and even things like scythes and pick-axes. True, there were some machine guns also, some modern rifles, and even artillery and a few aeroplanes, but woefully few compared with those of the efficiently equipped fascist forces.

Over the frontier, through Catalonia and on to Albacete went the international volunteers. The French and German sections had now grown particularly strong. At the training camps in and around Albacete men drilled under the direction of ex-officers from every army in Europe. They trained day and night. They drilled with wooden dummy rifles when they could not get the real thing. They worked sometimes by the light of guttering candles to acquaint themselves with the mechanism of machine guns.

They were training against time. Theirs was a race to bring aid at the last vital moment to a brave and sorely pressed people. And to save not only Spain, but eventually Europe from barbarism.

For the threat to Madrid at the beginning of November, 1936, was desperately close. The Government effort to push Franco's army back down theTagus Valley had failed—turned into a retreat. Of course it had failed. For two months the Government had been fighting without the tanks, artillery, aeroplanes and machine guns necessary to make it into a really formidable fighting force. For two months there had been a continual struggle to turn the thousands of untrained men of the new Spanish army into a disciplined military body capable of holding up the Italian and German military machines. Two months was not enough; you can't create a modern army in that time.

So Franco moved rapidly on Madrid. Right up to the very suburbs of Madrid. It became possible to take a bus or a subway train to the front line. From the taller buildings in the city you could see where the opposing armies were firing at each other.

Loud speakers were pouring out orders for the mobilisation of every available man. A Madrid newspaper issued a manifesto telling the women not to take their men's meals to the factories but to the front line trenches.

Leaflets were issued instructing the population how to

defend the houses and streets of the city against Franco's tanks and armoured cars. In blocks of flats committees of defence were being formed. " Every house a fortress," was the cry. That was a spirit that made the whole world wonder.

The fascists were jubilant. They saw themselves already controlling the greatest city in Spain—and the loss of Madrid would in those days have been a terrible blow; far greater than it would be to-day when an entirely different state of affairs exists.

General Mola had a white horse nicely groomed for his ride into conquered Madrid at the head of his troops. In a moment of ill-founded ecstasy General Franco told newspaper men that on the following day he would make a speech from the steps of the Ministry of the Interior. A premature—very premature—advance write-up describing the entry of the fascist army into the city was mistakenly released.

It was at this dark moment that what appeared to the people of Madrid to be a miracle happened. Into a city which was grimly, desperately preparing to resist street by street, house by house, life by life to the last bitter drop of blood, into that city there came, bringing brilliant hope, armed fighting men from every country of Europe. That was perhaps one of the most dramatic hours in world history. In such moments, by such men are humanity's misdeeds redeemed.

Some went up to the front in lorries, others marched through Madrid streets. Rank on rank they come, swinging along. Efficient looking men. Marching past crowds that watched them with an emotion almost too great for words.

Earlier they had passed through Valencia bringing encouragement to the Republican Government which had moved to that city from Madrid. Two years later Dr. Negrin, Prime Minister of Spain, recalled that day as he bade farewell to the international volunteers.

" International Brothers," he said, " you came to Spain of your own will, prepared to sacrifice your lives. I remember those grave moments in the month of November, when the whole world thought that Madrid would fall—Madrid, a defenceless city, except for the breasts of her sons.

" Never shall I forget the impression that I received at the sight of that solid marching column, resolute and defiant, as the first of the international volunteers marched through the streets of Valencia on the way to Madrid."

Among the defenders in Madrid when the main body of the International Brigade arrived was a group of British men. They and the others who were now arriving so quickly did magnificent work in University City and other sections.

The veterans formed a section of the machine gun company attached to the 2nd Battalion of the International Brigade. Alfred Brugers, French commander of the company, said:

" The British troops have given nothing but absolute satisfaction. Alike on the front and in the rest-camp their calm conduct is the best of the entire battalion. They have been praised for special valour by all the commanders of the company. How happy I should be if I could have a whole company made up of such men."

By December the British volunteers were arriving in hundreds. In some of the villages and towns through which the men had passed, children were singing " Tipperary," and " One, two, three, four, five, we'll get Franco dead or alive."

Early in January, 1937, when the fight outside Madrid was still dominating the war, the British Battalion was formed.

This was the foundation battalion of the XV. Brigade of the internationals which was later built up from British, American and Canadian battalions, each battalion including a proportion of Spanish soldiers.

Core of the British Battalion was the company that had already gained valuable experience on the Cordova and Madrid fronts—later to become the Major Attlee Company. Training had necessarily been hurried and intensive, for times were critical and men were needed. But this training, like that of the rest of the International Brigade, was unique. There was a spirit of co-operation and eagerness to learn. Battalion meetings were held for officers and men to discuss together methods of training, and here many suggestions valuable to efficiency were made.

D. F. Springhall, at that time political commissar of the Battalion, said later:

" It was because of many factors—the political consciousness of our men, their eagerness to attain the maximum military knowledge, their feeling that they belonged to a People's Army and were themselves helping to build up that army, their intense belief in their mission, the support they had from the population—that they were able later to prove themselves more than a match for the highly trained and better armed professional soldiers of the fascist invading army."

Those factors were indeed to stand them in good stead almost immediately, for their first engagement proved to be one of the fiercest that had been known up to that time—the battle of Jarama.

The fascists had nearly surrounded Madrid. Unable to take the city by storm, they hoped to cut every road and railway that carried food and ammunition to the besieged population and either to deprive them of arms or to starve them into subjection. Every road had been cut except the most vital of all—the famous Madrid-Valencia road. Along that road, so scarred by shells and bombs, came Madrid's supplies—the life-blood of the city. By that road Madrid was linked with the rest of Republican Spain.

To cut the Madrid-Valencia road the fascist forces were

straining every nerve—and the danger could not be denied. The British, French, German, and other battalions, pick of the International Brigade, were rushed up to hold the road. This was the British Battalion's introduction to front line fighting.

The British under the command of T. Wintringham went up to the front on February 12. Even as they were moving up the Italians were taking Malaga and beginning a massacre that shocked the world. The battalion knew nothing of those events, but news of Malaga's fall had reached the fascists and Moors on the Madrid front, sending their morale sky-high.

Aeroplanes, artillery, machine guns, bombs battered at the Republican lines; wave after wave of Moors and fascists attacked. After three days the inadequately armed Brigade fighters were forced back. The retreat looked almost as though it might become a rout, for men were beginning to move back in disorder.

Orders were given for the retreating forces to hold at all costs a ridge abutting on the main road and to make a new line there. But the troops were streaming away in scattered groups . . .

It was at this moment that the British Battalion proved itself —and the episode was one of the most gallant in its history. The Battalion, now commanded by Cunningham for Wintringham was wounded, had been scattered, like others, but it reformed itself into two halves and under a hail of fire marched from two different points along the road towards the ridge, singing the International.

It was a magnificent example. Retreating men saw two compact bodies of troops moving in good order towards instead of away from the advancing enemy. Groups stopped . . . rallied . . . joined the marching men. . . . More and more of them; back they went, back across open country under heavy fire, back to the ridge; reached the ridge . . . held the ridge . . .

They kept on holding the ridge. That piece of ground was never taken. And when dusk fell the battle took an entirely different turn. The Government troops, including the British

Battalion, counter-attacked along the whole front. The enemy broke, fled in disorganised retreats. They never got back near the Valencia Road. And to-day along that road still rumble lorries full of food, ammunition trucks—all that is vital for the defence of Madrid.

But the cost was terrible. Four hundred men were killed or wounded in the British Battalion. Four hundred of the best men this country ever saw.

Four months in the trenches at Jarama, with Fred Copeman now in command, a brief rest and then the Battalion found itself under a scorching sun at Brunete in July, 1937. Here in a terrible battle the Spanish Republican Army won successes that sent a thrill of encouragement through the whole of Government Spain. After three weeks of fierce fighting 80 square miles of ground was captured.

A " Message to the Comrades," issued on the eve of battle and signed by George Aitken, then political commissar of the British Battalion, said:

" To-day we are about to participate in the first great offensive of the new People's Army of Spain. For months we have borne the Spanish attack. Outnumbered and outclassed in armaments as we were, nevertheless they did not pass.

" The tragic farce of non-intervention denied the Spanish people its right to buy arms abroad, while Hitler and Mussolini openly poured men and munitions into the territory held by their puppet Franco. That is why our offensive has been so long delayed. But now our turn has come. . . ."

More recruits had arrived. The British Battalion went into action 300 strong. It came out with 42 men.

Brunete was taken by Spanish troops, lost, retaken, reduced by bombardment to something like a brickyard. As a town it existed no longer; it was only a position on a military map.

The British Battalion, with the Dimitrov Battalion, at Villa Nueva de la Canada; faced some of the fiercest moments of the fascist counter-attack, fighting a terrible rearguard action that caused it to sustain the heaviest losses in the XV Brigade.

The Brigade was in action continuously for more than three

weeks. The bombardment was terrible—trench mortars, heavy artillery and aeroplanes that had the sky to themselves. No wonder nerves began to wear thin after weeks of unrelieved struggle.

Walter Tapsell, political commissar, writing later, captured in vivid words the terror of those days:

" We had very few ' sick.' It was absolute and complete physical collapse, or else, ' Stick it, Jerry.'

" Men shaken and racked to the very soul, cursed and ground their teeth, and yet conquered the unimaginable terrors of broken nerves."

One section was taken out of the line for a rest. But there came a request for assistance.

" Someone," said Tapsell, " had to hold the line, and if it was a tough job, well we reckoned we were a tough mob, and the mob for a tough job. And if we felt like hell, then the fascists were not very happy. So the boys went back.

" Perhaps," adds Tapsell, " you are surprised to think that men can falter? But the real courage of these men was shown in that with all their courage and endurance they faltered and yet conquered themselves and went back to fight, more determined than ever."

So, from Brunete to the Aragon front and Belchite at the end of August, 1937. In this advance the People's Army captured Belchite and Quinto. Here the Battalion was better armed and its losses were comparatively light, but there were moments when, both flanks lacking support, it was in deadly peril.

The Battalion fought at Saragossa in October, but towards the end of the year when the fascist counter-offensive began against the positions so briliantly captured by Spanish troops at Teruel, it was once again moved to one of the most critical points of the war.

The month was December. Snow covered hills around Teruel were as bitterly cold as the plain at Brunete had been scorching. The battalion held and even improved its positions for three weeks until a final concentration of fascist forces and one of the most cruel artillery barrages that had yet been known forced a retreat.

There followed another comparatively quiet period, but in March, 1938, when Franco began his drive on the Aragon front, pushing through to the coast and threatening Catalonia every available man was hurried into action on this sector.

Those were dark days. The fascist wedge reached the sea, widened towards Valencia. Once again Franco and his supporters began to boast about the coming end of the war.

The Government troops were falling back before the weight of Italian soldiers and German and Italian arms. The British Battalion, like every unit, fought desperately. But it was particularly hard hit when in one attack Italian tanks advanced with unusual speed and captured a large number of men, including about 100 members of the Battalion.

By the beginning of April the Battalion had been reduced again to 70 men—the whole XV Brigade could only command 200. But on 2nd April the British, American and Canadian Battalions with the Spanish soldiers in their ranks made history. They occupied an important position on the Gandesa Road. To hold that position was vital, for behind was the main army falling back on the Ebro River, where terrible slaughter might well take place if Franco's men could push home their advantage.

The road was held. All day the Brigade stood to its guns. It repelled six tank attacks. It moved not an inch. And on the next day it was still there.

Behind, on the banks of the Ebro, the retreating army rejoined ranks, crossed the river, blew up the bridges, formed an unassailable line on the opposite bank.

In those days who knows how much was saved for Spain and freedom?

The Spanish Military Command addressed a message to the Army holding up the XV Brigade as an example for bravery, discipline and knowledge of how to prevent arms, men and munitions from falling into enemy hands.

The Republican Army dug itself in on the Ebro, paused to reorganise its forces, waited for fresh supplies and reinforcements and then launched its counter attack. Only just in time. For Franco was making headway in the coastal drive towards Valencia. But at the right time. For the main body of the fascist troops and arms had been thrown into that offensive.

The Republican Army suddenly crossed the Ebro River and hurled itself on the comparatively few of Franco's troops that had been left in that area. It was a surprise attack successful beyond expectations. Before the surprised fascists had time to bring reinforcements from the Valencia drive to face this new peril, Government troops were sweeping forward, had retaken most of the territory that had been lost. At the end of the first day's fighting the main body of troops found themselves a few kilometres south of Gandesa and 24 hours ahead of their planned time.

But fighting after that was stiffer. News of the attack had reached Franco's staff and the sky was darkened by Italian and German aeroplanes sent as the first reinforcement for the retreating troops. Then Franco, at the cost of discontinuing his Valencia offensive, managed to bring up more support. But the main purpose of the counter-attack had been gained —the threat to Valencia was removed.

The enemy aeroplanes were bombing to pieces bridges thrown across the Ebro, and for some time only a few Government tanks and heavy guns were able to cross. This meant that again the Government troops had to face superior armaments—a superiority which was even more pronounced

later when Franco's foreign artillery and tanks were rushed to the front.

On July 25 the British Battalion, led by Sam Wild, later decorated with the Spanish V.C., recrossed the River Ebro with the rest of the International Brigade; from that time until August 1—seven days—the Battalion fought without pause.

Like the rest of the Republican Army, they fought under the heat of the Spanish sun without water. They marched over hills and charged the enemy barefoot, for their shoes had been cut to pieces by sharp rocks; they fought in clothes that were only rags. From July 25 to July 30 they had little to drink and sometimes they went for a day without water, so sorely needed to moisten burning lips and parched throats.

It was at this time that they launched their famous attack on Hill 481. That hill was one of the few that had not fallen in the first rush of the Republican advance. Whoever held Hill 481 had a good chance of holding Gandesa—which was why the fascists had fortified it with what they believed to be impregnable defences. Concrete pill boxes dominated the slopes from the summit; machine guns commanded every approach. A battalion of reserves waited in the wooded slopes behind.

The principle attacks against Hill 481 took place on July 31 and August 1 when the men were already weary. The ordeal of those attacks is best described in the words of a man who took part—17 year old John Richardson, of Luton, writing to a friend:

" At dawn we went over the top. And the world went mad. Machine guns sent a hail of bullets at us, snipers shot at us, shells and trench mortars burst all around. But we reached cover at the bottom of the valley, where we lay all day, unable to move because of snipers.

" The heat of the sun became unbearable. The ground scorched and our clothes stuck to our backs. We had no water and my mouth and throat were swollen and hard with thirst. Still we lay there all day, then at last came the night and we were able to stretch our cramped and aching limbs.

" At 10 p.m. we got the order to attack. In a long line stretching along the side of the hill we crept up, carefully avoiding the mines tied to bushes, which all you had to do was to touch to get blown to pieces. We reached the very summit without a mishap. A little white later came the signal for the real business. We rose with a yell and rushed forward, throwing hand grenades as we ran.

" But the machine guns rained death at us. Red hot lead. Hand grenades burst all around. Time and time again we attacked, only to be driven back. The fortifications were too strong. Solid concrete pillboxes lined the hilltop and we were only flesh and blood.

" It was at this action that I got a hand grenade all to myself, and so I am writing this letter in hospital. Our company suffered terrible punishment . . . yet the company's morale was never shaken. They swore to take that hill if they had to carry it away in sacks.

" And I say it was worth while coming to Spain: for to see the way the International Brigade and our Spanish comrades went over the top was a revelation."

Twenty-seven British members of the Battalion and 23 Spaniards who had fought side by side with them were mentioned in dispatches after the battle. It was this action that gained for the British Battalion the title of " Shock Battalion of the XV Brigade."

And so on to the last battle of September 22—the very day when Dr. Negrin announced that the Republican Government had decided to withdraw all foreign volunteers.

On September 11 the XV Brigade had been moved into reserve, but later it had been hurried from point to point along the line, strengthening the weaker sections in moments of stress. President Negrin made his announcement on September 22 . . . and on that same day—but, again let a member of the British Battalion who took part in the fight tell the story.

Bob Cooney, political commissar, wrote:

" On the evening of September 22 our Brigade relieved the 13th, which had suffered severely. Our forces had not slept for three nights, and we were in a very exhausted state.

" We knew that we were due to be relieved the next night and that this would be our last action, as the Internationals were to be withdrawn. You can imagine how we felt. None of us could help but speculate on our chances of coming out alive, especially as we knew that we were going into a very dangerous position.

" Owing to the various delays it was daylight before we moved into the line and we had no time to take stock of our positions.

" What a day it was! Such artillery bombardments as I have never seen before. They literally churned up our position. Under cover of the artillery the fascists advanced with infantry and tanks. They were on top of us before we were aware of their advance. Our boys suffered heavily.

" We retired in as good order as possible and formed a line on the next ridge. The artillery bombardment, with continuous bombing from aeroplanes, continued. Somehow or other we managed to hold on till dusk, when we went to get our wounded. It took us four hours to do this, and then we were relieved. The following day we crossed the Ebro."

So the British Battalion, the oldest of the International Brigade, fought its last battle. So they left Spain. Along those roads, down which the first of them had marched in two's and three's two years before, they now went back.

In Barcelona thousands greeted the International Brigade. Those men who had fought so long, so hard, so self-sacrificingly for liberty now marched back behind the banners they had made glorious. Now they were no longer carrying rifles. Their arms were full of flowers. With flowers they were pelted. Men, women, girls, little children cheered them—cheered thanks as they had cheered greetings in those early days.

" Brothers of the International Brigade, come back. Spain will ever be your home," said banners that decorated their route.

The National Committee of the Popular Front sent a message which said: " We take our leave of you full of gratitude and with a profound feeling of fraternity. By your sacrifice and heroism you have become citizens of our country, and you will leave in the heart of every Spaniard a remembrance that will never be forgotten."

Andre Marty, organiser of the International Brigade, said: " Not Chamberlain and Daladier represent the people of Britain and France. It is the volunteers from these countries who represent the people of France and Britain. Let London and Paris be the first to give these men a reception worthy of the work they have done. Remember also that they will continue this work, and it is our duty to help them to do so."

A little more than a year earlier Evelyn Brown, wife of George Brown, a well-known Manchester man, had written when she heard of the death of her husband at Brunete:

" I know why George died. He died fighting back the advance of fascism because he loved freedom and the rights of the common people. He went to Spain because he knew that if we allowed fascism to conquer in Spain, very soon we should be having to face the guns of fascism in England.

" I feel that we should not play the Funeral March for such men as he was; surely the spirit of these boys of ours will never die.

J. C. Howarth, wounded in Spain, wrote to a friend:

"There's a lad I'd like to mention from Bristol. I say ' lad,' but he's 60, every bit of it, and was all through the last war. They call him 'Old Faithful.' They've tried to get him to go home dozens of times, but it's no use.

" The last thing he said to me was:—

" ' I came here to help the Spanish people fight for better times, and I ain't quitting.' "

No more than that could be said.

PHILIP BOLSOVER

Jarama Valley

Words by: Alec McDade, of Glasgow, killed at Brunete 6th July, 1938.

Tune: Red River Valley.

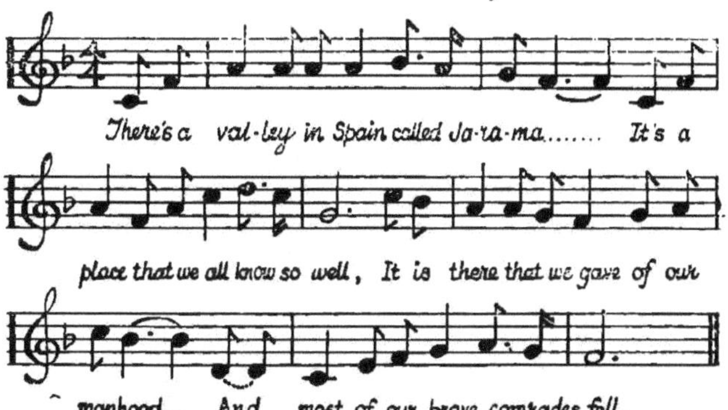

There's a Valley in Spain called Jarama,
It's a place that we all know so well,
It is there that we gave of our Manhood,
And most of our brave comrades fell.
We are proud of the British Battalion,
And the stand for Madrid that they made,
For they fought like true Sons of the Soil,
As part of the Fifteenth Brigade.
With the rest of the International Column,
In the stand for the Freedom of Spain
We swore in that Valley of Jarama
That fascism never will reign.
Now we've left that dark valley of sorrow
And it's memories we ne'er shall forget,
So before we continue this reunion
Let us stand to our glorious dead.

*

Alec McDade was a native of Glasgow and at the time of his death was assistant Company Commissar of the British Battalion. He was undoubtedly one of the best liked men in the Battalion and he did great work whilst he was in Spain.

*

Anti-Tank Battery

In the spring of 1937, when the Spanish Government acquired some of the newest and most efficient light-artillery pieces in the world, the Internationals were called on to form the first batteries for their use. One of these was the Anglo-American Anti-Tank Battery, which after a brief and hurried training, hauled its guns up to the lines at Jarama, and in the quiet June days in that sector got to know itself and its guns and feel pride in both.

The battery had three guns, called Anti-Tank guns, because one of their functions was to destroy advancing tanks. They had other uses, the most important of which, so far as this battery was concerned, was the elimination of medicine gun nests preparatory to an infantry advance. For a shock brigade like ours, taking part in one offensive after another, this was an essential service.

We learned beneath Mosquito Crest, the vital point in the Brunete battle, what the job was really like in active warfare.

We first experienced an air bombardment, when a squadron of fascist bombers went for us as we were driving up to take our first positions with the infantry battalions. We did not see them coming. The first we knew was that bombs were roaring in a ploughed field about 50 yards to the right of us. A second's difference in the timing and most of us would have closed our experience of real war where it began. The first artillery shells to be fired at us landed right beside their mark before we knew the fascists had even seen us. While we were waiting for final instructions, near Brigade headquarters, the worst barrage of the war up to that time came over at us while we crouched in a shallow trench.

In this battle we had little time or energy left to let these things depress us. We changed our positions continually, firing from positions behind the lines, in them, sometimes even in front of them. The physical effort of dragging those guns and the ammunition up the rough, steep hills of that terrain was greater than any of us had thought possible to sustain. In that dusty soil it ground the soles off our feet.

Nobody who was in that battery in the Brunete days will forget the morning that followed our withdrawal from the sector into a reserve position. We went down to bathe in a nearby river. Sitting in the shallow water, we sang like a bunch of children. Our spirits were high.

In time it became a byword in the XIth Brigade that you couldn't get the Anti-Tank Battery down. Our reputation was up to anyone's, and a matter of pride to every man. For this, good leadership was largely responsible. Malcolm Dunbar and Hugh Slater were our first two commanders—none better. Bill Alexander was our political commissar before he left to become adjutant of the British Battalion. Otto Eslensen, Arthur Nicoll and Alan Gilchrist carried on their tradition. These men not only gave us good military and political direction, but were wise enough to encourage our cultural activities as well at times when there was opportunity for them, and our wall newspaper, "Assault and Battery News," achieved, we were told, a reputation among the best in the Spanish Army.

The Battery saw service in all the Brigade's campaigns until March, of 1938, when massed fascist artillery knocked out our guns at the beginning of their push through Aragon down to the Ebro. By the time we were ready to hit back and cross the river again, the remaining members of the battery had been drafted into the British Battalion, and played their part there with the best. There lie some of the best of them now.

Ours was a fine unit, and we shall not forget it. Those of us who have come back will see to it that its spirit stays alive.

MILES TOMALIN.

Hospital Interlude

In February of 1938, when the Battalion came from Teruel to go into rest, a number of men were sent to the English Convalescent Hospital at Valdeganga for rest and medical attention for various minor complaints which needed care.

Thirty arrived on Sunday night. Thirty grimy, cold, hungry men. All had lice, infected feet, coughs and colds. They had been in the lines for more than three weeks, with no shelter from the bitter weather, from the snow and wind. During those weeks they had not tasted warm food nor drink, since their position had made it impossible for the food kitchen to be set up near the lines, and by the time their food had reached them it had always been more than an hour on the way. During those weeks they had not been able to wash nor shave, nor to have any of the medical attention they needed.

All of us in Valdeganga rushed to minister to them. We were so proud to have them in our hospital, and so anxious to be able to help them. Spanish and International staff and patients ran to help. We boasted a bath-house in Valdeganga of which we were very proud; within half an hour the water was hot and relays of men set off for the bath-house, each with a piece of our much-cherished English soap and a change of clothing. Later, one by one, clean men, almost unrecognisable as the bearded, tired ones of a little earlier, emerged and sat down to a meal.

It did one good to see their faces as the warmth and good food and cleanliness did their work. We spent the evening singing and talking, and closed the recreation room earlier than usual, so that the English boys could get a good rest, in their first beds, between the first sheets, for many a long month.

In the morning, everyone in the hospital felt the cheerful necessity of working harder than usual that day because of our new guests, for whom nobody could do too much. But to our surprise, when they had seen the doctor and received medical treatment, all of them joined in the work of the hospital. Some helped the kitchen staff; the mechanically minded ones soon found their way to the garage, and began helping in the work that constantly needed to be done to keep our ambulances and food trucks in good condition; the majority of them joined the group which had been working for days on the construction of a new and larger dining-room, and more progress was made that day than had been made in three weeks before.

The clothes were put into disinfectant. Women came up from the nearest village to offer to give us help with the extra washing. A small committee formed itself of the different language groups to plan a concert for the following night. A food-wagon set off in search of such extra food as could be found in the surrounding countryside. A bustling, hospitable feeling pervaded the whole hospital. Everyone had a plan for making the stay of the English boys a pleasant one.

At the end of the first day we went to bed still happily thinking of the days before us and the things we planned to do. Before all of us were asleep, however, a car drove to the hospital and a Commandante came seeking the Administrator.

"In half an hour," he said, "a lorry will come and call for the English you have here. They have to go back to the lines to-night."

With grief in our hearts we went round to their rooms and called them out of bed. None of them needed much wakening. Soon they were lining up in the corridor, silently, so as not to wake the patients, We were horrified to realise that all the warm clothing they had discarded was still soaking in disinfectant, to rid it of the lice, and we had no other clothing to give them than the thin summer shirts and trousers with which we had temporarily supplied them. Hastily we went round the hospital searching for spare blankets for them to wrap themselves in. Not one man uttered a word of complaint. One, who at his medical examination had been thought to be suffering from gastric ulcers and had been marked down for an X-ray examination the following day was told to fall out and stay behind.

"I refuse to stay," he said briefly.

"You b—— well fall out," said the officer in charge.

"I refuse to stay," came the reply again.

We searched for food, so that they could take some rations with them. Alas, there was very little. But what we had we gave them. There would be no breakfast for the patients in the morning, but we knew they would not care.

The lorry came. Quietly and quickly they gave us farewell, climbed into the lorry, and drove away. We stood in the cold bitter snow watching them disappear, and wondering how many of these heroic men we should ever see again.

NAN GREEN.

¡NO PASARÁN!

Vol. II • SPECIAL No. 9 — Barcelona, March 17 • 1938

¡NO CEDER UN SOLO PALMO DE TERRENO AL ENEMIGO!

DO NOT YIELD AN INCH OF GROUND TO THE ENEMY!

Defend every conquered position; hold our lines firmly; FORTIFY, FORTIFY, FORTIFY, THIS IS THE DUTY OF EVERY SOLDIER

> Brigadas Internacionales, congregación generosa y espontánea de hombres de las Cinco partes del Mundo, que pedían una plaza para morir por la libertad.
>
> DR. JUAN NEGRIN

GUADALAJARA

HACE UN AÑO

En Guadalajara el enemigo poseía instrumentos de combate numerosos, mejores y mayores que los nuestros entonces. Sin embargo, fué primero contenido y después aplastado.

El factor decisivo de aquel gran episodio, como tiene que serlo junto a nuestros mejores elementos de combate en la lucha de mañana, fué la MORAL INQUEBRANTABLE DE NUESTROS SOLDADOS la firmeza, la decisión y el coraje de nuestros MANDOS Y COMISARIOS POLITICOS.

A YEAR AGO

In Guadalajara the enemy possessed more numerous and better weapons than ours then. However, first the enemy was held back, then beaten.

The decisive factor of that great episode, was the brilliant morale of our troops, the strength, the courage of our commanders and Political Commissars. With this same Morale we can Smash Through the Fascist Offensive and hold high Banner of the Republic.

Defender bien cada posición conquistada, mantener fuertes nuestras líneas. FORTIFICAR, FORTIFICAR, FORTIFICAR, es el gran deber del soldado, mandos y comisarios.

> Ayuda a los Comisarios para que no exista un solo combatiente que ignore para que lucha y que es lo que va a ganar con la victoria.

These Men Led

Major Nathan went to Spain in September, 1936. He had had previous military experience as an officer in the British army. Commanded the First Company of the Dumonde Battalion on the Madrid and Cordoba fronts. Later became Staff Officer of the 15th Battalion, then Commandant of the 11th Battalion of the 14th Brigade. Then returned to the 15th Brigade as Chief of Staff. Major Nathan was killed at Torra le Donas.

Wilfred McCartney went to Spain in October, 1936. Served on the Madrid front, and returned to Madisgueras in December, 1936. He commanded the 16th Battalion during its training at Madisgueras, and was militarily responsible for the organisation of the first British Battalion. Returned to England in March, 1937.

Tom Wintringham went to Spain in October, 1936. Was Machine Gun instructor during the formation of the Battalion, and Battalion Commander from February 10, 1937. Was wounded at Jarama and Belchite. Commanded the Officers' Training School at Posorubio. Returned to the Brigade as Brigade Staff Officer. Was wounded during the Belchite offensive, after which he returned to England.

Jock Cunningham went to Spain in September, 1936, Served on all fronts—took over command of the Battalion on February 15, 1937. A very courageous military leader. Was wounded in March, 1937, returned as Chief of the Sector commanding the British, American and French Battalions of the Brigade. Returned in England in October, 1937, after distinguished service for the Republic.

Fred Copeman went to Spain in December, 1936, and was Machine Gun Instructor for the Battalion during training. Wounded at Jarama. Returned to the Battalion as Adjutant in March, 1937, then became Battalion Commander. Led the Battalion through Jarama actions and Brunete. Returned to England in August, 1937, for a propaganda campaign. On return to Spain he became Staff Officer of the 15th Brigade. Took over the Battalion for the second time from October, 1937. Returned to England in April, 1938.

Charlie Goodfellow went to Spain in January, 1937. Second in Command of No. 3 Company, later became Adjutant during the Jarama and Brunete offensives. Killed at Brunete on July 8, 1937. A member of the Coachbridge Branch of the Communist Party—a sincere and gallant fighter.

Joe Hinks was one of the first Britishers to go to Spain. He served in the Dumonde Battalion, in University City, and on all other fronts. Joined the British Battalion in June, 1937—became Adjutant, and for a short time Battalion Commander. One of the few Britishers who have served with the Chinese People's Army, he was in the 29th Regiment at Chapei, Shanghai, during the Japanese attack in 1932.

Bill Meridith—or Ronald Denis—was a member of the Bellingham Labour Party. Battalion runner in the Jarama action, he became Company Commander of No. 2 Company. Gave long and consistent service to the Spanish Republic. Killed at Brunete on the evening of July 6th—while helping a wounded fascist he was treacherously shot in the back by the fascist officers.

Pat Daley served with the 86th Brigade at Cordoba. Later returned to the British Battalion, with whom he was killed at Quiento on the Aragon front in September, 1937. A member of the Irish Republican Army, he was a well-known fighter for Ireland's Independence.

Harry Fry joined the Battalion in January, 1937—became Commander of No. 2 Company. Captured at Jarama—after many months in Franco prisons, he returned to England.

Finally rejoined the Battalion, and was killed whilst leading men at Mediana, Aragon.

Paddy O'Daire was with Pat Daley in the 86th Brigade on the Cordoba front. He joined the British Battalion in September, 1937, and led the Battalion at Belchite, at Quiento and Mediana. Later became Commander of the Major Attlee Company. Returned to England with the Battalion in December, 1938. A well-known fighter for Irish Independence.

George Fletcher joined the Battalion in July, 1937—became Commander of the Machine Gun Company. Later led the Battalion at Fuentes de Ebro. Wounded many times. Later became Adjutant of the Battalion until its withdrawal. A comrade who gave long, consistent service to the People of Spain.

Bill Alexander — a research chemist — was originally Political Commissar of the Anti-Tank Battery, but joined the Battalion in October, 1937, as Adjutant. Led the Battalion at Teruel, Alfambra. Wounded on the Aragon front. Returned to England in October, 1938.

Sam Wild went to Spain in December, 1936. Was wounded at Jarama—rejoined the Battalion and later became Company Commander of No. 1 Company. At Brunete was again wounded. In April, 1938, he became Battalion Commander. Awarded the highest military award for valour by the Spanish Government. Returned with the Battalion in December, 1938.

George Aitken was the first Political Commissar of the British Battalion in action. He went to Spain in January, 1937—a member of the Amalgamated Engineers Union, well-known in North East England. He later became Political Commissar of the 15th Brigade, and held this position through the Jarama and Brunete actions. Returned to England in October, 1937.

Walter Tapsell—first business manager of the "Daily Worker"—went to Spain in March, 1937. Attached to the Political Commissariat until June, he joined the Battalion as private. Later became Battalion Commissar. Went through Brunete offensive, Teruel, Mediana, and Belchite. Killed at Caleceite, March, 1938.

Bert Williams went to Spain in March, 1937, and was attached to the Political Commissariat of the 15th Brigade. Later, he became Political Commissar of the Battalion, on the promotion of George Aitken to the Brigade. Returned to England after the Brunete offensive. A well-known leader of the working class movement in the Midlands.

Councillor Bob Elliot—member of the Blythe Town Council. Was Political Commissar of No. 2 Company from the formation of the Battalion until his death at Brunete on July 8. His memory will be loved and cherished by all who had the honour to serve with him. His undying faith in the working class was an inspiration to the whole Battalion. He died at he lived—in the struggle.

Eric Whalley went to Spain in April, 1937. A member of the Independent Labour Party, he later joined the Communist Party. Became Political Commissar of the British Battalion after Bert Williams. Was killed by the side of Harry Fry at Quiento. A young and enthusiastic fighter for freedom.

FRED COPEMAN.

Such Men Died

In the ranks of the British Battalion were six men from almost every walk of life. From the long roll of honour we single some out as examples of the type of men who were willing to sacrifice everything for democracy, and whom fascism destroyed. As you read about them, remember their many comrades—men of talent and accomplishment—men who knew how to work and fight for progress in this country —who gave their lives in Spain.

JIMMY RUTHERFORD

Was among the first men from Britain to fight for the Spanish Government.

He came of fine old stock. His family had been associated for generations with the Society of Free Fishermen of Newhaven. He was a great favourite there especially in the Fish House, where he worked with David Dryburgh, the Newhaven trawlerman, who is president of the Society of Free Fishermen and Parliamentary candidate for Labour in Leith.

When he was just 19 years old—November 1936, Jimmy went to Spain to aid a cause which had always been dear to his heart. He was captured by Franco and sentenced to death. He joked to keep his fellow prisoners cheerful, even while he expected his own death at any moment. But he was released at the last moment in an exchange of prisoners.

Returning to England he conducted a campaign of aid for Spain. Then, this young boy—only 21—went back to fight for his ideals, knowing full well he would be shot if recaptured.

He was recaptured, was recognised, and shot.

RALPH FOX

Fox was killed on 3rd of January, 1937, near Lopera, Andalusia, where the fascists were making a drive to gain the rich olive groves of Jaen.

He came of a comfortable middle class family. He was a

well-educated and cultured man. When he left Oxford, a prosperous, aloof literary career seemed open to him.

Instead he went with a famine relief expedition to South East Russia. What he saw there made up his mind for him. He joined the Communist Party. He wrote, worked and taught alongside the working man. When the time came, he fought for liberty in Spain, as Byron did in Greece, and Landor in Italy.

As Harry Pollitt has said: Instead of mellowing gradually into a literary editor, he died at thirty-six, fighting the forces of Fascism in Spain.

His presence in Spain was proof of his readiness to combine practice with theory, to act as he believed. His death is proof of his willingness to sacrifice everything for the struggle against fascism, and for culture and liberty.

To those writers and others who would like to stand aside from the everyday struggle of the people, Fox has addressed these words (he is writing of our cultural heritage, that "spiritual community binding together the living and the dead," as Wordsworth called it):

> *"Our fate as a people is being decided to-day. It is our fortune to have been born at one of those moments in history which demand from each one of us as an individual that he make his private decision . . . We are a part of that spiritual community with the dead of which Wordsworth spoke. We cannot stand aside. And by our action we shall extend our imagination, because we shall have been true to the passions in us."*

JOHN CORNFORD

John Cornford was a professor's son, a brilliant student, and a poet, who promised to be one of the best in the country.

Though very young, he had been a most prominent leader of the student movement for some years, and his efforts, more than those of any other single individual, helped to forge the unity of the Left wing student organisations.

Cornford was one of the first international volunteers

to arrive in Spain. In the early days of the war, he was on the Aragon front, later he took part in the defence of Madrid. He was a vital personality, a brave soldier and a great comrade; and he was killed on the Cordoba front on his twenty-first birthday.

Before the storming of Huesca, Cornford wrote: —

Though Communism was my waking time,
Always before the lights of home
Shone clear and steady, and full in view—
Here, if you fall, there is help for you—
Now, with my Party, I stand quite alone.

Then let the private battle with my nerves,
The fear of pain whose pain survives,
The love that tears me by the roots,
The loneliness that claws my guts,
Fuse in the welded front our fight preserves.

O be invincible as the strong sun,
Hard as the metal of my gun,
O let the mounting tempo of the train
Sweep where my footsteps slipped in vain,
October in the rhythm of its run.

WALTER TAPSELL

Walter Tapsell's brilliant business ability was for six critical years devoted to building up the "Daily Worker." He joined its staff in 1931, as Business Manager, and with tireless energy travelled up and down the country building solid foundations for the paper's present circulation.

A good disciplinarian at work, a delightful companion with a vast fund of entertaining conversation, "Wally" was loved and respected by the whole "Daily Worker" staff, many of whom he trained in their jobs. When he joined the Brigade in February, 1937, his going meant a great loss to the " Daily Worker." The news of his death has left a deep sense of grief and pride in the whole working class movement.

LEWIS CLIVE

The death of Lewis Clive cut short a brilliant career of sport, academics and politics. Educated at Eton and Christ Church, Clive rowed No. 6 for Oxford in the University Boat Race in 1930 and 1931. In 1932 he won the doubles sculls for England in the Los Angeles Olympic Games.

Before going to Spain he worked with the New Fabian Research Bureau, wrote a book on " The People's Army " (as an ex-Guardsman), and was elected Labour Councillor in North Kensington.

DAVID GUEST

David Guest was another outstanding example of a leading academic career ended by fascism. Guest was educated at Oundle and Cambridge, where he took first-class honours in Mathematics. In his life at home, however, he took his full share in the working class movement. Son of Islington's Labour M.P., Doctor Hadon Guest, he was for years a delegate to the Trades Council and member of the Youth Advisory Committee.

In one of his letters home, Guest wrote: " I have myself a lively desire to explore whole fields of theoretical work, mathematical, physical, logical. . . . But, of course, this is not possible now—' to-day the struggle ! ' "

CLEM BECKETT

Known in the Speedway world as Dare-Devil Beckett, Clem was perhaps the most brilliant rider to be seen on the tracks in the early years of the sport.

In all ways he was a great chap. I know of no other way he would have sooner given his life than by fighting for the working people.

Almost as soon as the Fascist menace showed its face he

was in Spain. His work with the International Brigade had the value of great experience and also a clear knowledge of the issues of the struggle.

A few years ago I knew him very well indeed, as he used to be a member of the British Workers' Sports Federation and stayed with me when he made trips to London.

Beckett was the first Speedway rider to introduce the sport in the Soviet Union, for in 1931 he went with a delegation of athletes to Moscow and other parts.

His exhibitions on the improvised tracks thrilled the Russian workers in the extreme, and so well did he perform, and so enthused were the fans of his daring and skill, that he was induced to remain behind for further exhibitions, while the rest of the delegation came home.

He was a man of iron determination and deep character. Words did not come easily to his mouth, but what he said was weighted with reason.

All athletes and readers will raise their hats in homage to this great sportsman and fighter.

George Sinfield,
" Daily Worker " Sports Editor.

PHIL RICHARDS

Phil Richards, before he joined the International Brigade, was a popular feather and lightweight boxer—" one of the best fighters I have known in the ring," as Albert Hicks, member of the National Union of Boxers, called him, at the memorial meeting to honour him.

Mr. Johnny Sharp, well-known boxers' manager, said he was proud to be at a meeting to give respects to a real fighter.

" Phil was an idealist," he said, " the kind prepared to lay down his life for his ideals."

Phil's brother said: " My brother died fighting a monster, and I hope all people will open their eyes to that monster, and fight it, too."

BRITISH BATTALION

XV

INTERNATIONAL BRIGADE

ROLL OF HONOUR

Cordova
Jarama
Brunete
Belchite
Saragossa
Teruel
Aragon
Gandesa
Ebro

Aaronberg, M. Sheffield—Jarama—February, 27, 1937.
Addley, H. (C.P.). Folkestone—Boadilla—December 12, 1936.
Airlie, F. Newcastle—Ebro—July 30, 1938.
Alexander, John. Dundee—Brunete—July 16, 1937.
Alwyn, J. Bolton—Jarama—February 1937.
Armstrong, A. (Y.C.L.). Manchester—Jarama—Feb. 27, 1937.
Atkinson, J. (C.P.). Hull—Jarama.
Avgherinos, C. (C.P.). London—Jarama—April 30, 1937.
Avner, S. (Y.C.L.). London—Boadilla—December 20, 1936.
Allstop, G. Rotherham—August 30, 1938

Bailey, Wm. Hawood—Jarama—June 1937.
Ball, W. (C.P.). Reading—Jarama—February 27, 1937.
Banks, W. Paticroft, Lancs.—Ebro—August 30, 1938.
Barry, J. (C.P.) (Australia). Madrid—December 1936.
Beales, W. Newport, I.O.W.—Ebro—August 30, 1938.
Beattie, W. Belfast—Brunete—July 16, 1937.
Beaton, John W. Glasgow—Ebro—August 8, 1938.
Beckett, Clem (C.P.). Oldham—Jarama—February 1937.
Beadles, R. Birkenhead—Jarama—February 1937.
Bennett, C. A. (C.P.). Walsall—Ebro—July 26, 1938.
Berry, John (C.P.). Edinburgh—Jarama—February, 1937.
Bibby, L. (C.P.). London—Jarama—February 1937.
Birch, Lorimer (C.P.). London—Boadilla—Dec. 20, 1936.
Bird, A. E. (C.P.). London—Brunete—July 9, 1937.
Black, John D. (Lab. Party). Dover—Brunete—July 7, 1937.
Black, John G. Glasgow—Brunete—July 17, 1937.
Bolger, B. London—Jarama—May 1937.
Bond, K. P. (C.P.). London—Ebro—July 27, 1938.
Bonnar, Alec. Glasgow—Jarama—February 27, 1937.

Boswell, Bruce (C.P.). Coventry—Ebro—July 1938.

Boyce, Wm. Teruel—January 29, 1938.

Bradbury, K. (C.P.). Oldham—Teruel—January 1, 1938.

Brannan, Thos. Blantyre—Jarama—February 1937.

Bright, George (C.P.). London—Jarama—February 1937.

Briskey, Wm. (C.P.). London—Jarama—February 1937.

Bridges, Robt. Leith—Jarama—February 1937.

Breedon, S. A. London—Ebro—July 31, 1938.

Brent, Wm. Barnsley—Ebro—August 30, 1938.

Broadbent, Clement (Labour Party). Dewsbury—Ebro—September 9, 1938.

Browne, Felicia (C.P.). London—Aragon—November 1936.

Browne, George (C.P.). Manchester—Brunete—July 1937.

Brown, W. J. Newmilns—Jarama—February 1937.

Brown, Frank. Prestwick.

Bruce, John. Alexandria—Jarama—February 27, 1937.

Bogle, W. Liverpool—Jarama—February 27, 1937

Bonar, Henry. Dublin—Cordova—December 1936.

Bonar, Hugh. Dungloe, Ireland—Jarama—February 27, 1937.

Boyce, W. G. Bristol—Teruel—January 1938.

Burke, T. Glasgow—Brunete—July 7, 1937.

Burke, E. (C.P.). London—Cordova—January 1937.

Burton, J. Bristol—Jarama—February 23, 1937.

Cameron, D. Glasgow—Jarama—February 14, 1937.

Campbell, J. London—Jarama—February 1937.

Campeau, G. (C.P.). London—Jarama—February 1937.

Canaris, A. C. (C.P.). London—Brunete—July 1937.

Casey, Francis (C.P.). Glasgow—Jarama—February 1937.

Cantrovitch, R. (Y.C.L.). Manchester—Brunete—July 1937.

Caplan, P. (C.P.). London—Brunete—July 1937.
Capps, A. (C.P.). London—Teruel—January 20, 1938.
Carter, T. J. (C.P.). W. Hartlepool—Jarama—Feb. 2, 1937.
Cassidy, Jas. Glasgow—Jarama—February 1937.
Charlton, P. Leeds—Jarama—February 17, 1937.
Clive, Lewis (C.P. and L.P.). London—Ebro—Aug. 1, 1938.
Cockburn, Jas. London—Cordova—January 1937.
Cody, Dennis. Dublin—Las Rosas—January 1937.
Cohen, Jack (C.P.). Liverpool—Jarama—February 1937.
Coles, Wm. (C.P. and L.P.). Cardiff—Jarama—Feb. 1937.
Connolly, J. (Y.C.L.). Glasgow—Jarama—February 27, 1937.
Conroy, F. Dublin—Cordova—December 28, 1936.
Conway, Chris. (C.P.). Dublin—Jarama—February 1937.
Coomes, J. (C.P.). London—Aragon—October ?
Cornford, J. (C.P.). Cambridge—Cordova—Dec. 28, 1936.
Cormack, C. London—Ebro—July 31, 1938.
Cox, Wm. London—Jarama—February 1937.
Cox, Ray. (C.P.). Southampton—Boadilla—Dec. 20, 1936.
Craig, A. Glasgow—Jarama—February 1937.
Craig, George (S.D.F.). Ulmanston—Jarama—Feb. 1937.
Crawford, W. J. (C.P.). Glasgow—Jarama—February 1937.
Coombie, F. (C.P.). Kirkcaldy—Brunete—July 16, 1937.
Coutts, R. N. Shields—Jarama—February 1937.
Cunningham, Jas. (C.P.). Glasgow—Ebro—August 20, 1938.
Curley, Pat. Dumbarton—Jarama—February 1937.

Daglish, J. Leith—Jarama—February 3, 1937.
Daley, Peter (C.P.). Wexford—Saragossa—September 1937.
Davidovitch, M. (Y.C.L.). London—Jarama—February 1937.
Davie, Adam. Glasgow—Jarama—February 1937.

Davies, W. J. (C.P.). Tonypandy—Brunete—July 19, 1937.
Davies, Harold. Neath—Jarama—February 1937.
Davis Wm. Ireland—Brunete—July 1937.
Deegan, Vincent. Brighton—Ebro—August 30, 1938.
Deegan, G. (Y.C.L.). Balloch—Teruel—January 1938.
Dewar, A. Aberdeen—Ebro—August 30, 1938.
Dewhurst, P. (C.P.). London—Brunete—July 11, 1937.
Dickinson, E. A. London—Jarama—February 1937.
(Taken prisoner and shot by fascists)
Dickson, W. J. Prestonpans—Brunete—July 17, 1937.
Dobson, H. (C.P.). Rhondda—Ebro—July 31, 1938.
Dobson, Walter. (C.P.). Leeds—Ebro—August 30 1938.
Docherty, Frank (C.P.). Glasgow—Ebro—July 31, 1938.
Dolan, John. Glasgow—Jarama—February 1937.
Dolan, Thos. Sunderland—Jarama—February 1937.
Dolling, Chas. London—Brunete—July 1937.
Donaldson, W. Glasgow—Teruel—January 28, 1938.
Donelly, Chas. Glasgow—Jarama—February 1937.
Doran, A. (L.P.). Weston-super-Mare—Jarama—Feb. 1937.
Douglas, J. Glasgow—Jarama—February 1937.
Drinkwater, F. Burnley—Brunete—July 10, 1937.
Duffy, Jas. (Y.C.L.). Glasgow—Ebro—August 30, 1938.
Dunbar, A. London—Brunete—July 10, 1937.
Duncan, Richard. Scotland—Flix—September 6, 1938.
Durkin, Martin. Middlesbro—Ebro—August 30, 1938.

East, Lionel. London—Aragon—March 31, 1938.
Edelman, Sydney (C.P.). London—Ebro—August 30, 1938.
Elliott, R. S. (C.P.). Blyth—Brunete—July 1937.

Elius, P. (C.P.). Leeds—Jarama—February 1937.
(Taken prisoner and shot by fascists)
Evans, E. A. (C.P.). Glasgow—Aragon—March 15, 1938.
Elliot, Thos. (*L.P.*) Worthing—Jarama—June 1937.
Esteban (C.P.). Abercrave.

Fairchild, J. (C.P.). London—Ebro—August 30, 1938.
Fellingham, J. (C.P.). Bury—Teruel—January 20, 1938.
Felton, R. (C.P.). Rochester—Jarama—February 13, 1937.
Fink, Sydney (Y.C.L.). Salford—Aragon—March 1938.
Fisher, Jas. Buckhaven—Jarama—February 1937.
Flecks, Thos. (C.P.). Blantyre—Jarama—May 27, 1937.
Flynn, J. F. (Y.C.L.). Glasgow—Cordova—April 7, 1937.
Foxall, C. L. Sale—Jarama—February 1937.
Fox, Ralph. (C.P.). London—Cordova—December 28, 1936.
Fox, Wm. (L.P.). Blantyre—Jarama—February 7.
Francis, Archibald (C.P.). Reading—Aragon—March 1938.
Francis, S. London—Teruel—January 17, 1938.
Freedman, F. London—Teruel—January 20, 1938.
Fretwell, George (L.P.). Penygroes—Jarama—Feb. 12, 1937.
Fry, Harold (C.P.). Edinburgh—Fuentesdel Ebro—Oct. 13, 1937.

Gallaher, M. Wigan—Brunete—July 1937.
Gibbons, Thos. (C.P.). London—Brunete—July 1937.
Giles, W. J. (Y.C.L.). Liverpool—Jarama—February 1937.
Gilmour, J. Prestonpans—Jarama—February 1937.
Glacker, Pat. (L. P.). Greenock—Teruel—January 20, 1938.
Glasson, Pat. Redruth—Brunete—July 20, 1937.
Gold, A. (Y.C.L.). London—Jarama—February 1937.
Gomm, H. (C.P.). London—Jarama—February 1937.

Goodfellow, Chas. (C.P.). Bellshill—Brunete—July 1937.

Goodison, Michael. Salford—Ebro—August 30, 1938.

Goodman, R. (Y.C.L.). Nottingham—Jarama—Feb. 1937.

Goodman, W. R. (Y.C.L.). Salford—Jarama—February 1937.

Gough, W. J. (C.P.). Luton—Boadilla—December 20, 1936.

Grant, T. (J. P. Burley). Nottingham—Aragon—March 1938.

Gross, Harry (C.P.). London—Brunete—July 16, 1937.

Grossart, D. (C.P.). Glasgow—Jarama—February 1937.

Guest, David (C.P.). London—Ebro—July 26, 1938.

Gura, Mark (C.P.). London—Jarama—February, 1937.

Guerin, E. London—Saragossa—August 1937.

Hamill, T. Glasgow.

Hamm, Sid (C.P. and L.P.). Cardiff—Brunete—July 10, 1937.

Hall, Alex. Plymouth—Ebro—August 1938.

Hall, John. Rutherglen—Aragon—March 10, 1938.

Hardy, Geo. (C.P.). London—Aragon—April 1938.

Harding Jas. Stockton-on-Tees—Ebro—Sept. 23, 1938.

Harkins, Jos. Clydebank—Ebro—July 26, 1938.

Harris, A. (C.P.). Liverpool—Brunete—July 10, 1937.

Harris, J. (C.P.) Llanelly—Jarama—February 1937.

Harvey Alex. Glasgow—Jarama—February 13, 1937.

Hempel, Martin (C.P.). London—Ebro—July 31, 1938.

Henderson, David. Glasgow—Jarama—February 1937.

Henderson, Jas. London—Brunete—July 17, 1937.

Henderson, Richard. Kirkcaldy—Ebro—August 30, 1938.

Henry, Wm. Belfast—Jarama—February, 1937.

Hickman, Ivor (C.P.). Petersfield—Ebro—Sept. 24, 1938. (Wound.)

Hilliard, R. M. (C.P.). Falmouth—Jarama—February, 1937.

Halloran, D. Middlesbrough—Jarama—February, 1937.
Hoare, Arnold. Leeds—Ebro—August 30, 1938.
Horradge, D. (L.P.). Huddersfield—Brunete—July 1937.
Hone, Roger. Hammersmith—Ebro—August 30, 1938.
Huson, Leslie (C.P.). Bristol—May 1938.
Hunt, V. J. London—Brunete—July 1937.
Hyman, C. Glasgow—Jarama—March 30, 1937.
Hyndman, Jas. (C.P.). Glasgow—Las Rosas—January 1937.

Jackman, E. Liverpool—Jarama—February 14, 1937.
Jackson, G. Cowdenbeath.
Jasper, W. E. London—Jarama—February 19, 1937.
Jobling, Wilf. (C.P.). Blaydon-on-Tyne—Jarama—Feb. 1937.
Johnson, W. (C.P.). Newcastle—Cordova—December 1936.
Jones, D. J. Rhondda—Jarama—February 27, 1937.
Jones, T. H. Aberdare—Ebro—August 1938.
Jordan, L. (Y.C.L.). Manchester—Brunete—July 14, 1937.
Jordan, R. P. Wembley—Ebro—March 1938.
Jeans, Arnold (C.P.). Manchester—Boadilla—Dec. 30, 1936.
Julius E. (C.P.). London—Aragon—November 1936.
Jones, Jas. (C.P.). Harrow-London—Ebro—July 1938.
Jones, H. F. (C.P.).
Jackson, Wm. Oldham—Ebro—August 30, 1938.
Jones, E. (C.P.). Madrid—December 1936.
Jones, Thos. (C.P.). Wrexham—Ebro—September 17, 1938.

Katsonaris, A. (C.P.). London—Jarama—February 1937.
Keegan, W. (C.P.). Glasgow—Brunete—July 1937.
Kelly, Michael (I.R. Congress). Kilconnel, Ireland—Brunete —July 8, 1937.

Kenny, W. (Y.C.L.). Manchester—Jarama—February 1937.

Kemp, A. Glasgow—Teruel—January 30, 1938.

Kent, J. New Zealand—Drowned s.s. City of Barcelona—June 1937.

Kermode, Jas. (C.P.). Milngavie—Cordova—January 1937.

Kerr, Thos. Belfast—Vich Hosp. (Typhoid)—Oct. 10, 1938.

Kerry, A. London—Brunete—July 1937.

Killick, T. F. Southport—Jarama—February 1937.

Kirk, R. Liverpool—Jarama—February 1937.

Knottman, Jas. (C.P.). Manchester—Cordova—January 1937.

Lacey, Clifford (Y.C.L.). London—Ebro—Sept. 23, 1938.

Langmead, W. (L.P.). London—Brunete—July 1937.

Large, L. G. (L.P.). London—April 1938.
(Died of exposure as prisoner of war)

Larlham, C. A. London.

Langham, James. Motherwell—Brunete—July 1937.

Laughlin, W. Belfast—Brunete—July 1937.

Laws, Harold (C.P.). Southampton—Teruel—Feb. 1938.

Lawther, Clifford. Hexham—Jarama—February 1937.

Ledbury, D. A. (C.P.). Swansea—Ebro—July 1938.

Lee, Samuel (Y.C.L.). London—Jarama—February 1937.

Lees, Jos. (C.P.). Oldham—Brunete—July 1937.

Legge. Rosyth—Ex-prisoner (Typhoid)—Nov. 10, 1938.

Leppard, A. (Y.C.L.). London—Jarama—February 1937.

Leslie G. S. (C.P.). London—Brunete—July 1937.

Litchfield, A. (C.P.). London—Ebro—July 1938.

Livesay, M. (C.P.). London—Segovia—June 1937.

Lomax, R. K. (C.P.). Shrewsbury—Jarama—Feb. 1937.

Lower, W. E. Sunderland—Drowned " s.s. City of Barcelona "—June 1937.

Lyons, Jas. (C.P.). Glasgow—Jarama—February 1937.

Mackie, R. H. (C.P.). Sunderland—Brunete—July 1937.

Mandell, M. (C.P.). London—Brunete—July 1937.

Marlow, I. A. R. (C.P.). London—Jarama—February 1937.

Marks, A. (Y.C.L.). London—Brunete—July 1937.

Marshall, James S. (C.P.). Clydebank—Ebro—Aug. 30, 1938.

Maskey, Bert (C.P.). Manchester—Jarama—February 1937.

Masters, Sam (C.P.). London—Brunete—July 1937.

Mason R. Edinburgh.

Maugham, Leslie. London—Teruel—January 1938.

May, M. Ireland—Cordova—December 28, 1936.

Meehan, J. Galway, Ireland—Cordova—December 1936.

Mennel, Cecil. London—Teruel—January 1938.

Meredith, W. (C.P.) (Bob Dennison). Glasgow—Brunete—July 1937.

Messer, Martin (Y.C.L.). London—Boadilla—Dec. 20, 1936.

Miller, M. (C.P.). Hull—Ebro—August 1938.

Moir, Jas. (C.P.). Perth—Brunete—July 1937.

Moore, Th. (C.P.). Manchester—Teruel—January 1938.

Morice, Ken. (C.P.). Aberdeen—Ebro—July 1938.

Morris, Wm. (C.P.). Llanelly—Brunete—July 1937.

Morriss, Phil (L.P.). London—Jarama—February 1937.

Morriss, Sam. Ammanford—Brunete—July 1937.

Muir, A. (C.P.). London—Jarama—February 1937.

Murray, Ben (C.P.). London & Ireland—Aragon—Mar. 1938.

Murray, Joe. London—Aragon—March 1938.

Murray, Wm. (C.P.). Glasgow—Brunete—July 1937.

McCabe, A. (C.P.). Bootle—Brunete—July 1937.
McCabe, F. Dundee & London—Brunete—July 1937.
McCulloch, F. Glasgow—Aragon—October 1937.
McDade, Alex. (C.P.). Glasgow—Brunete—July 1937.
McDonald, R. Glasgow—Drowned s.s. "City of Barcelona" —June 1937.
McDonald, Donald (C.P.). Brighton.
McElroy, Jas. Wishaw—Jarama—February 1937.
McEwen, G. Liverpool—Jarama—June 1937.
McGregor, Alec. London—Teruel—January 1938.
McGregor, Wm. S. (C.P.). Dublin—Ebro—Sept. 23, 1938.
McGrotty, Eamon. Dublin—Jarama—February 1937.
McGuire, E. (Y.C.L.). Dundee—Jarama—February 1937.
McKeown, A. Glasgow—Brunete—July 1937.
McKay, David (Y.C.L.). Glasgow—Ebro—August 30, 1938.
McKissock, J. (C.P.). Glasgow—Jarama—April 1937.
McKie, Wm. London—Ebro—August 30, 1938.
McLanders, J. Dundee—Jarama—April 1937.
McLaughlin, F. Newmains.
McLaurin, G. C. (C.P.). Cambridge—Madrid—Dec. 1936.
McLeod, Chas. Aberdeen—Ebro—August 1938.
McMullan, W. Bellshill—Teruel—January 1938.
McManus, Tim. London.
McNally, A. (C.P.). Birmingham—Aragon—March 1938.
McWhirter, Thos. Glasgow—Aragon—March 1938.

Nalty, J. (C.P.). Dublin—Ebro—September 23, 1938.
Nash, Max (Y.C.L.). London—Ebro—July 1938.
Nathan, A. S. London—Brunete—July 1937.
Ness, J. (C.P.). Dundee—Ebro—July 1938.

Newbury, F. Manchester—Jarama—February 1937.
Newman, J. Liverpool—Jarama—February 1937.
Newsome, Arthur (C.P.). Sheffield—Cordova—January 1937.
Nolan, Michael. Dublin—Cordova—December 1936.
Norton, F. (L.P.). Liverpool—Jarama—February 1937.
Nuns, M. (Emile Pezaro) (C.P.). London—Aragon—March 1938.
Norbury, J. T. (C.P.). Liverpool—Jarama—February 1937.

O'Brien, Thos. T. Liverpool—Jarama—February 1937.
O'Brien, Francis (C.P.). London—Teruel—January 1938.
O'Day, Peter (C.P.). London—Aragon—March 15, 1938.
O'Neill, R. (C.P.). Belfast—Jarama—February 1937.
Oldershaw, T. (C.P.). Battersea—Aragon—March 1938.
O'Sullivan, P. (C.P.). Dublin—Ebro—July 1938.
Overton, Bert. Stockton—Brunete—July 1937.
Owen, Frank (C.P.). Mardy—Brunete—July 1937.
Owens, J. D. Liverpool—Jarama—February 1937.

Palmer, G. London—Cordova—January 1937.
Palzeard, J. South Shields—Jarama—February 1937.
Parkes, A. Manchester—Brunete—July 1937.
Patton, Tom. Dublin—Madrid—December 1936.
Paul, E. (C.P.). London—Jarama—February 1937.
Pearson, H. C. H. (C.P.). London—Ebro—July 31, 1938.
Perdikon, D. (C.P.). London—Jarama—February 1937.
Perry, Leonard. London—April 1938.
(Died in Saragossa Hospital)
Petterson, J. Liverpool—Ebro—August 30, 1938.
Pitman, J. (C.P.). London—Jarama—February 1937.

Porter, A. (C.P.). Manchester—Jarama—February 1937.
Proctor, F. J. Liverpool—Ebro—August 1938.
Plumb, F. A. (C.P.). Luton—Jarama—February 1937.
Pryme, L. G. (C.P.). London—Ebro—August 1938.
Picton, Thos. (C.P.). South Wales.
(Killed as Franco Prisoner)

Quinton, Frank (C.P.). London—Morata—June 1937.
Quinlan, M. P. Waterford, Ireland—Jarama—February 1937.

Rae, Jas. (Y.C.L.). Glasgow—Jarama—February 1937.
Rawson, H. (C.P.). Oldham—Cordova—December 1936.
Redmond, J. (C.P.). Liverpool—Aragon—March 1938.
Reynolds, H. Newcastle—Jarama—February 1937.
Ross, John (C.P.). Edinburgh—Aragon—March 1938.
Rowney, W. C. (" Maro ") (C.P.). London—Jarama—February 1937.
Rickman, John (C.P.). London—Jarama—February 1937.
Redhill, J. Glasgow—Aragon—October 1937.
Riley, John. Glasgow—Teruel—January 1938.
Riordan, J. E. (C.P.). London—Ebro—August 30, 1938.
Robinson, A. L. Blackhall, Co. Durham—Aragon—Oct. 1937.
Robilliard, Victor. Dagenham—Ebro—October 11, 1938.
(Died of wounds)
Rodriquez, R. (C.P.). Dowlais, S. Wales—Brunete—July 1937.
Ryan, Maurice. Ireland—Ebro—August 1, 1938.
Ryder, Ed. London—June 1938.
(Died, wounds, prisoner of war)

Samson, D. Dundee—Brunete—July 1937.
Scott, H. G. London—Jarama—February 1937.

Seal, Wm. (C.P.). London—Jarama—February 1937.
Segal, Nathan (C.P.). London—Cordova—December 1936.
Seligman. U.S.A.—Jarama—February 1937.
Shammah, V. (C.P.). Manchester—Aragon—March 1938.
Shields, J. Glasgow—Jarama—February 1937.
Sherpenzeel, Jack. London—Ebro—July 31, 1938.
Silcock, Thos. Liverpool—Jarama—February 1937.
Sim, Ernest. Aberdeen—Ebro—September 8, 1938.
Simmons, C. J. Portsmouth—Jarama—February 1937.
Smith, Malcolm (C.P.). Dundee—Ebro—August 1938.
Smith, W. Birkenhead—Aragon—March 1938.
Smith, J. (C.P.). Irvine—Ebro—September 8, 1938.
Smith, David. Glasgow—Jarama—February 1937.
Smith, H. J. (C.P.). Gateshead—Jarama—February 1937.
Sollenberger, R. London—Brunete—July 1937.
Spencer. Pontefract—Jarama—February 1937.
Sprigg, Christopher S. (C.P.). Claygate—Jarama—Feb. 1937.
Sproston, Walter (C.P.). Manchester—Calaceite—Mar. 1938.
Stalker, Ken. (C.P.). London—Jarama—February 1937.
Steele, John (C.P.). Falkirk—Jarama—May 1937.
Steigman (C.P.). London—Jarama—February 1937.
Stevens, J. (C.P.). London—Jarama—February 1937.
Stevens, J. E. (C.P.). Australia—Brunete—July 1937.
Stevenson, Jos. (C.P.). Scotland—Typhoid—February 1938.
Stockdale, George. Leeds—Ebro—July 1938.
Straney, Jas. Belfast—Ebro—July 1938.
Strangward, H. J. P. (C.P.). Onllwyn—Ebro—August 1938.
Strickland, L. A. London—Jarama—February 1937.
Stott, Maurice (C.P.). Rochdale—Jarama—February 1937.

Swindells, E. (C.P.). Manchester—Jarama—February 1937.
Sylvester, Jack (Y.C.L.). London—Jarama—February 1937.
Sykes, Fred (C.P.). Leicester—Jarama—February 1937.
Symes, R. (C.P.). London—Madrid—December 1936.
Tadden, John. Dundee—Jarama—February 1937.
Tagg, H. (C.P.). Doncaster—Jarama—February 1937.
Tapsell, Walter (C.P.). London—Calaceite—April 1938.
Tattam, Wm. (C.P.). Whitburn, Durham—Brunete—July 1937.
Taylor, J. London—Jarama—February 1937.
Thomas, Brazell (C.P.). Llanelly—Ebro—July 1938.
Thomas, J. G. J. (C.P.). Gillingham—Jarama—Feb. 1937.
Thompson, A. Durham—Teruel—January 1938.
Traill, R. London—Brunete—July 1937.
Tumilson, Liam. Belfast—Jarama—February 1937.
Turnill, F. (C.P.). Worksop—Teruel—January 1938.

Unthank, J. (C.P.). Middlesbrough—Jarama—Feb. 1937.

Walsh, David. Ballina, Ireland—Teruel—January 1938.
Walsh, S. E. (C.P.). Liverpool—Jarama—February 1937.
Walsh, S. E. (C.P.). Newcastle-on-Tyne—Brunete—July 1937.
Warbrick, F. (C.P.). London—Aragon—March 1938.
Ward, R. Manchester—Jarama—June 1937.
Wark, J. Airdrie—Jarama—February 1937.
Watson, Wm. Glasgow—Aragon—February 1938.
Watts, Roy (Y.C.L.). Leicester—Ebro—September 23, 1938.
Webb, W. A. (C.P.). London—Jarama—February 1937.
Westfield, G. Liverpool—Aragon—October 1937.

Whalley, Eric (C.P.). Mansfield—Fuentes Delebro—October 1937.

Whalley, John (C.P.). London—Aragon—March 1938.

Whitehead, F. (L.P.). Manchester—Jarama—Feb. 1937.

Wheeler, Jas.

White, F. (C.P.). Ogmore Vale—Brunete—July 1937.

White, J. London—Jarama—February 1937.

Williams, J. E. (C.P.). Ammanford—Brunete—July 1937.

Wilkinson, E. F. (C.P.). Sunderland—Jarama—Feb. 1937.

Wilkinson, Norman. Manchester—Jarama—February 1937.

Winfield, D. G. (Y.C.L.). Nottingham—Teruel—Jan. 1938.

Winter, A. (C.P.). Glasgow. Brunete—July 1937.

Wise, H. London—Cordova—January 1937.

Wolstencroft, E. (C.P.). Oldham—Aragon—March 1938.

Woods, Thos. Dublin—Cordova—December 1936.

Yates, Anthony (Y.C.L.). Gasgow—Jarama—February 1937.

Yates, Stephen (Y.C.L.). London—Boadilla—Dec. 1936.

Zamorra, F. (C.P.). Abercrave—Teruel—January 1938.

" To all those who have gone, we say on behalf of the people of Britain, who will one day come to understand the great and glorious task you have undertaken, thank you, comrades! We shall not forget your work; your sacrifice is, and shall for all time be, a glorious example to us all."

*

International Brigade Graves at Suen Carrall, Madrid.

Letters

Dear Mother,

"... But seriously I am more convinced than ever that I was right to come. To live at such a time as this and take part in so magnificent a struggle is the greatest honour that can call to anybody. This is one of the most decisive battles ever fought for the future of the human race and all personal considerations fade into insignificance by the side of it. . . ."

"As a humble member of the International Brigade, who was not offered ten pounds a week to come to Spain, but who came here freely of his own accord, it is very gratifying to hear that you folks in England are doing so much.

"Without in any way underrating the good work already done in England, it is well to realise that the rousing of public opinion to such a strength as to force the powers that be to intervene, is far better than ambulances.

"I have been in hospital for a small operation which has been quite successful.

"Two days ago I was given the chance of going to Murcia (and eventual evacuation to England) or back to 'El Frente.'

"You won't need any telling that I plumped without hesitation to go back to 'The Boys,' for while Spain remains in her agony from 'International Fascism' I could never rest outside of the acual fight.

"After being in the thick of the fighting for the Government, I have found that everyone I came in contact with—French, British, American or any other nationality—held in common the view that to fight for democracy in Spain is to help the cause of humanity everywhere.

Dear Olive,—Even if you have not heard from mother, you will see from the stamp on this letter that I am in Spain.

"... Now I want to explain to you why I left England. You will have heard about the war going on here. . . .

"From every country in the world working people like myself have come to Spain to stop Fascism here. . . .

"So although I am miles away from you, I am fighting to protect you and all children in England as well as people all over the world.

"I hope you can understand this note, also I will never forget you while I am in Spain.

"I know you will do your best to pass your examination. Write soon. A letter will be very welcome from you. Best love, Daddy."

Dear Dad.—I am very sorry you have got wounded rigt through the calfe of your left leg. Well here is some more good news to tell you that I can ride my bike. I learnt in five minutes, uncle Jack taught me how to ride.

You may know there was a spanish Flag day in England mom and me sold in it. Now mom said she would like to come to Spane for a holiday after the ware is over and I ageed.

Will you please send me a Spanish pence.

Mom said you are very brave to go. Signed—Peter to dad.

"I know why he died. He died fighting back the advance of Fascism, because he loved freedom and the rights of the common people. . . . We should not play the Funeral March for such men as he. Surely the spirit of these boys of ours will never die." From Mrs. George Brown.

"It was a sad blow to us to receive your letter regarding the death of our son and brother out in Spain. Whilst it has left a gap in our home, we feel proud that his death shall be a monument in the fight for democracy of which he believed. He knew what he was doing."

From the family of Brazell Thomas of Llanelly who was killed during the Ebro offensive.

"Many thanks for the photograph of my dear son's grave. I hope the day is not far away when I shall be abl to go and see his last resting place. That day will be when his comrades have swept the Fascist murderers out of Spain. My family are happy to know that Wille and his comrades are not forgotten."

From Mrs. McGuire whose son, William, was killed at Jarama.

"We fight solely for our principles, and the only reward we seek is the final defeat of Fascism that machine-guns women and children from the air.

". . . going home under those conditions would be a betrayal of those of our comrades who lie beneath the olive trees.

"We gave them a solemn promise that they would be avenged, and I want to see that vengeance accomplished. . . . We have lost many comrades . . . good men and true men. . . ."
Anti-Fascist greetings, Ben.

back to their positions because of their own barbed wire & there was a terrible slaughter as our machine guns opened up on them. Our last day in the line saw very heavy fighting & we lost several of our lads & at night we were relieved. We marched right through the night in order to reach our rest position for it is not possible to march in day time due to enemy aviation. We are now at rest, but it is not the rest what one can picture. We still have the enemy aviation over us the best part of the day & we hear the crashing of artillery for we are not very far from the front.

For the next 5 or 6 days we shall have a rest & reorganise & then once again back "up the line," to fight the hordes of international fascism. It is a hard life & I dont suppose that I will ever get used to it. but it has to be done & our lads are doing it. It is the same old tale of the lack of war material but in spite of our handicap our victory will be won.

I have not had a letter from you for a long time & I wish you would write & let me know how the A.U.U is getting on etc. Well I will close now sending my best regards

Remember

Wherever you go, whoever you meet amongst the fighters and workers for Spanish liberty as against tyranny, thank them in our name. Their good cause must spread throughout the length and breath of the world.

Ebby Edwards.

Then our 15th Brigade came abreast, and as I saw our proud Battalion banner, with the names of every battlefield, from Madrid to the Ebro inscribed on it, I thought:—

"Will the British workers, who are soon to be reading these names, understand that the men who died in each of these battles, died fighting to save our liberties in Britain?

"Will the British people realise that the men who survive are worthy of a welcome in Britain no less great than this mighty farewell in Barcelona to-day?

"These are the men who saved the good name of our country."

The last of the Internationals had passed, and pouring along behind, not waiting to permit the last of the procession to join up, came the workers of Barcelona—men, women and girls in spontaneous demonstration.

The sun was setting in a great fiery orb. Its almost horizontal rays picked out the marching workers, while a strong, cold wind, precursor of the winter, swept the leaflets and flowers up and chased them along the street.

As we joined the masses of people below, the chill of the night was ever more pronounced, because of the previous excitement.

The Spanish people are facing the rigours of their third winter as the Internationals leave. But we know that their promise will be made good. They will make good the promise, emblazoned on their banners along the route: "Brothers of the International Brigade, come back; Spain will ever be your home!"

So down the road we marched, and when we came in sight of the bridge we observed a body of men about fifty strong on the side of the road. . . . About fourteen of them carried me on to the road with rifles pointing at us, shouting "Manos arriba!" They then lined us up and started frisking us for guns.

There we were, stood up reaching for the sky, when I happened to catch Bobby Walker's eye.

"What are they, Sam, fascists?" said Bobby. I nodded. "O.K." he whispered "Yes," I said, "Let it go."

Then wham! Bobby's fist elevated the chin of the nearest fascist and then the fun started. I kicked the legs from under one, Dobson hit one with a tin of bully in a sandbag and everybody in a bunch contributed to the free fight. We all managed to get away, with the exception of young Sanchez, Bobby had to swim the Ebro and finished on the road naked, but nevertheless O.K. The remainder of us are still arguing which of us beat Jesse Owens' record.

A few minutes went by in which I gave him injections, etc., then he said, "if you can, Penny, tell Pollitt that the people in Britain must work."

With these words and his hands restfully in mine, Major Nathan died quite peacefully, like a true comrade of the Spanish people.

"A column of silent marchers two thousand strong, showed yesterday the deep love that Battersea has for those of its sons who have died during the fighting of Spain."

"Battersea's men, they were for Spain!
Spain's men, they fought the whole world's fight!
Register, drums, half pride, half pain!
Speak for the dead, that lived life right."

News Report Sept. 12 1938.

A raw young volunteer was receiving tuition in bomb throwing from an instructor. After everything had been carefully explained to him, he was given a live bomb and told to throw it.

He pulled out the pin and and handed the bomb to his instructor, remarking:

"Well, and what do I do now?"

He was so deeply offended at the reply he received that he reported the instructor for using bad language.

"It was like hell let loose. Tanks, planes, shells, machine-guns and hordes of Germans and Moors coming across in masses. Our boys were fine, fighting like tigers for every inch of ground."

— When did Franco say he was going to enter Madrid?

— Oh, that was long before your time.

"Harry Pollitt arrived on Christmas Day when the festivities were well under way, and he was received with a tremendous burst of cheering. Every man saw in him not only one of the best friends of the British Battalion, but also the representative of the people of Britain. He made a short, moving speech of greeting which aroused us all to great enthusiasm and renewed the marvellous reception he had earlier been given.

We had a good old-fashioned Christmas, complete with puddings and chickens and various little presents. Even the absence of beer was hardly noticed, as it was replaced by liberal supplies of wine and champagne.

Everyone felt very grateful to the people of Britain who had sent out the parcels that helped to make this Christmas like a day in the country.

The Teruel victory dominated festivities organised by the British Battalion, inspiring great enthusiasm and confidence."

(News Report)

The Marching Song of the 2nd Company of the British Battalion.

Yes we ken the traitor Franco,
Who's found he could not stay,
He lived at Burgos,
Once on a day,
But now he has gone
Far, far away,
For he fled to Salamanca in the morning.

The Company Commissar was harassed. The boys had been beefing; the grub line was snarled up and sounded like the Chicago stockyards in a thunderstorm.

Up walks Comrade S... Said he to the Company Commissar. "Was there any mail for me to-day?

"Comrade S. . .", said the C.C. "You know damned well that if there had been, I'd have seen that it got to you. You know damned well how anxious I am for the men to get their mail."

"Well," said Comrade S. in a forlorn voice, "It's beginning to get serious now."

The C.C. was harassed. "Serious" he snorted. "Whaddye mean, serious? I'm getting sick of you guys beefing about the mail. How long since you've had a letter? How long, eh?"

"Well," said Comrade S. . . in a small voice, "it's been nine months now."

C. R. Attlee, leader of the Parliamentary Labour Party, spoke to English, American and Spanish soldiers of the International Brigade when he visited their quarters yesterday, leading an official Labour Party delegation which included Ellen Wilkinson and Philip Noel Baker. The First Company of the British Battalion received the honorary name of Major Attlee Company.

Mr. Attlee then spoke to the assembled Battalion as an old soldier. "We have seen and we know the spirit of the Spanish people," he said, "and like you are sure of their victory."

"We promise in the name of the entire delegation to take the truth of the struggle back to the English people and to do everything in our power to try to bring pressure to bear to change our policy so fraught with danger to democracy."

Of non-intervention he said "It should have been over long ago. Everybody knows it is a farce."

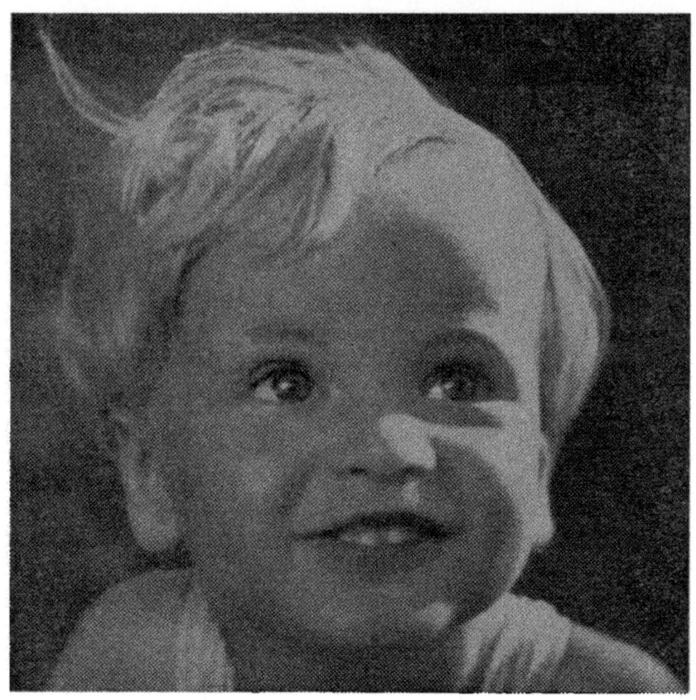

They had Faith in us . . .
we cannot betray that trust

One of the great factors in helping to keep up the magnificent morale of the British volunteers in Spain was the knowledge that their loved ones at home were receiving the material support necessary and regularly. Under the patronage of a number of leading representative people of all sections of the democratic movement, a Committee was formed to raise the necessary funds to ensure this.

Later, when the many battles took their toll, the question of the care of the returned wounded appeared, and the Committee extended its work to provide medical and hospital treatment with maintenance until recovery could be assured.

In this great work the Committee and the Battalion have had the support of all sections of the British public.

Working mainly on a voluntary basis, the Committee has raised £43,358 in a period of eighteen months, ending November 30th, 1938.

The Trade Union Movement has subscribed £7,432. Pride of place must be given to the miners who have never failed to help when the assistance was most needed.

In hundreds of factories and offices, weekly collections have raised £5,885. Again without slighting any other of our supporters, we must specially mention the workers of Odhams and Marlboro Press who have contributed nearly £1,500.

Unselfish work by Spanish Aid Committees brought £5,908 whilst over a quarter of the fund came from individual donors who understood the great rôle the Brigade was playing in the fight for civilisation.

With the repatriation of the Brigade, the work of the Committee is not ended. At some time or other three out of every five of the men were wounded. Many of these will not work for months; others are incapacitated for life.

These, with many orphans, constitute a responsibility which the whole of British democracy will shoulder.

Thus, in honour of the 500 British men killed, a £50,000 Memorial Fund has been inaugurated. This Fund will be used to ensure that not one wounded man nor orphan child shall want and that the debt of gratitude we owe to the men will be shown in our care of the fatherless and the crippled.

The great love of the British people for those who carried on the traditional fight for freedom is a sure guarantee for the future.

We, the undersigned, willingly support the proposals of the Wounded and Dependants' Aid Committee appeal for £50,000 to meet the future need of the wounded and families of the men who have fallen:

Signed:

Sir Norman Angell
Lieut.Col. Maurice Alexander, C.M.G., K.C., B.C.L., B.A.
Richard Acland, M.P.
C. R. Attlee, M.P.
Harry Adams (A.U.B.T.W.)
Vernon Bartlett
Rev. A. D. Belden, B.D., D.D.
Arthur W. Brady (Sec. Glasgow Trades and Labour Council)
Alfred Barnes, M.P. (Ch. Co-operative Party)
H. N. Brailsford
Isabel Brown
Air Com. L. E. O. Charlton, C.B., C.M.G., D.S.O.
Dean of Chichester
Professor R. H. S. Crossman
Prof. F. M. Cornford,, F.B.A.
F. Seymour Cocks, M.P.
E. F. Carritt, M.A.
A. J. Cummings
Ven. F. L. Donaldson, M.A., Canon of Westminster
John Langdon-Davies
Sidney R. Elliott
Hamilton Fyfe
V. M. Finney
Victor Gollancz
Milner Gray, C.B.E.
Alex Gossip (Sec. N.A.F.T.A.)
Jim Griffiths, M.P.
Oliver Harris (Sec. S.W.M.F.)
Prof. J. B. S. Haldane, F.R.S.
G. Maurice Hann (Sec. S.A.U.)
Arthur Horner (Pres. S.W.M.F.)
John Jagger, M.P.
E. McKnight Kauffer
J. C. Little (President A.E.U.)
Will Lawther (Sec. D.M.A., Vice-President M.F.G.B.)
Professor Harold Laski
Professor H. Levy, M.A., D.Sc., F.R.S.E.
Lord Listowel
Leah Manning
Tom Mann
Naomi Mitchison
Sir Peter Chalmers Mitchell, C.B.E., F.R.S., F.Z.S., D.Sc., LL.D.
Henry Nevinson, LL.D.
Sean O'Casey
Harry Pollitt
John Parker, M.P.
Lord Parmoor
D. N. Pritt, K.C., M.P.
J. B. Priestley
Paul Robeson
A. Maude Royden, C.H., D.D.
J. Rowan (Sec. E.T.U.)
Wilfrid Roberts, M.P.
G. R. Strauss, M.P.
E. Shinwell, M.P.
W. J. R. Squance (Secretary A.S.L.E. & F.)
Dame Sybil Thorndike, D.B.E., LL.D.
Sir Charles Trevelyan
Alfred M. Wall (Sec. L.S.C.)
H. G. Wells
Ellen Wilkinson, M.P.
Ted Willis (Ch. League of Youth)

Send contributions to Charlotte Haldane, Hon. Sec. Wounded and Dependants' Aid Committee, 1, Litchfield Street, W.C.2. Telephone: Temple Bar 0178.

As the Train Steamed in...

At last the train steamed into Victoria Station, and from its windows there waved the flags of fifty-two nations. Even before it stopped, mothers and sons, wives and husbands were reunited.

As they left the train, headed by Battalion Commander Sam Wild, Political Commissar Bob Cooney and Quartermaster "Hookey" Walker, they were welcomed by Mr. Attlee, leader of the Labour Party. With him were Mr. Will Lawther of the Miners' Federation, Mr. William Gallacher, M.P., of the Communist Party, Mr. J. R. Squance, Railmen's leader, Sir Norman Angell, Lord Strabolgi, Sir Stafford Cripps and Tom Mann. (*Daily Worker*, Thursday December 8.)

Led proudly by their wounded comrades, the men marched into London. With them marched the spirit of Byron, the Tolpuddle martyrs, the Chartists, Keir Hardie. . . Britain's bravest fighters for liberty through the centuries. . . Behind and around them marched twenty thousand British democrats.

Men as well as women wept and cheered alternately. It was no political affair, for all parties were represented, both on the platform and in the crowd. It was British democracy spontaneously expressing its abhorrence of Fascism and its appreciation of bravery.

These men have made history, by forming part of the greatest international democratic army the world has ever known. They have inspired the world by their example. Something of this seemed to enter into everyone who was at Victoria last night, and the memory of it will never be eradicated. (*Star*, Thursday December 8.)

When it was all over, and the station was almost quiet again, the oldest porter to be found was asked if he had ever seen anything like this

"No," he said, "I saw nothing like it even at the end of the last war." (*News Chronicle*, Thursday, December 8.)

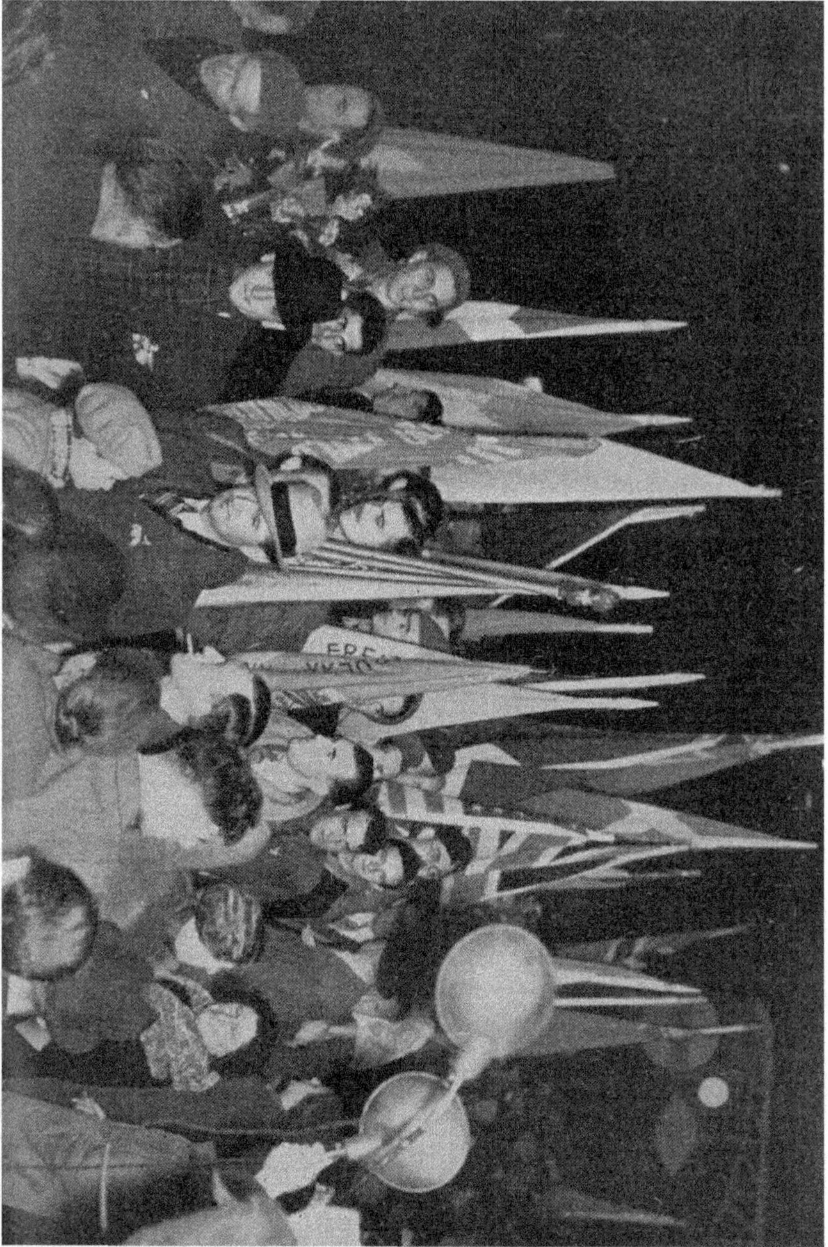

Are you glad to be back?

" Are you glad to be back ? " they've been asking us. " You must be glad to be back ! " When you haven't seen your family and friends for twelve, eighteen, twenty months, of course you're glad to be back. When you have been feeding thinly on duck-peas and lentils, it's good to have your wife or mother overfeed you. When you have been dodging bullets, shells, and bombs in all weathers, from burning heat to bitter cold, you appreciate a few creature comforts.

It's good to have eggs and bacon for breakfast, and to meet your old pals over a pint in the local.

Yes, that lasts for a few days, and then the novelty dies down. Now the difficulties begin to stick out. What about a job ? What about A.R.P., and the National Register, and Chamberlain selling out one country after another to the very men you have been fighting ?

"You should stay in Spain if you want a comfortable life," wrote a friend in England to a member of the XVth International Brigade, at the time of the recent crisis. "It is impossible to live in England now, the way things are going, and it looks as if in a short time Spain will be the safest corner of Europe."

But Spain found herself strong enough to fight without the International volunteers, and to show the world that the Spanish people were fighting under no Government's orders but their own, they withdrew those men that had come to help them in their moment of greatest need, and had taught them how to build an army.

And so we English came home to a country that is still enjoying the comforts of peace—a country where you can buy cigarettes, chocolate, milk round any corner, and the sky is not filled with the black wings of fascist aviation.

The contrast was immense. It hit us with a jolt, and when the first days of excitement had passed, it seemed almost a shameful thing for us to be enjoying even these simple comforts when our friends in Spain, who had cheered us on our last march through Barcelona with such a grand warmth and enthusiasm, were at this very moment entering on a winter of privation and hardship worse than we had ever known.

I spoke to a woman soon after I came back. She said: "War is horrible. Why did you have to go and join a war that had nothing to do with you? Why couldn't you let Spain work out its own troubles by itself? After all, England is different." I answered her: "If Spain had been left to work out her own troubles from the start, there would have been no need for anybody to go. The Spanish people never wanted

fascism, least of all to-day. But, thanks to somebody, those who wished to invade and conquer Spain have been given a free hand to do so, and if you want to know who that somebody is, it's the man who governs this different England of yours."

I was angry enough to say a lot more, but the woman hadn't seen what I had seen. She didn't really grasp what was going on. I told her how I had listened to Spaniards speaking of the England of Mister Chamberlain, and how for the first time in my life I felt downright ashamed of my country. England is different? Very well, then, England is blind and Spain can see—that's the difference.

" Pobre Inglaterra " runs the text of a song they sing in

Spain; " Poor England! she tries to cut our throats and only succeeds in cutting her own."

When we left Spain, we promised the Spanish people that we would carry on the fight for them at home with at least as much resolution and energy as we had shown on the Spanish battlefields. It wasn't just a sentimental fancy. We weren't feeling sentimental, and we aren't now. It isn't only that we want to see justice done to a brave and generous people. There are folk in England whom we have loved all our lives, and to see them suffer as we have seen helpless Spaniards suffer, will be worse for us than the worst we have seen. If the fascists were to conquer Spain, these same horrors, larger, more brutal still, if that is possible, would be creeping nearer and nearer to England.

It must not happen. As long as these men are governing Britain who have not only allowed, but encouraged, the fascists down the road of aggression that ends among the ruins of our own homes, we, the British volunteers of the International Brigades, will fight them. In some ways we have the most difficult actions yet to face. We have changed our front and changed our weapons, that is all.

The promise we made to the people of Spain will be respected. To this we now add another, a promise to the people of Britain. We, who know the horror, the degradation and the suffering of war, pledge ourselves to do all in our power to save our own people from it. Our fight for world-peace is carried on now under the flag not of Spanish but British democracy. Those who in the name of " government " are betraying the traditions of democracy sacred to the British people are our enemies. We will fight them in the name of peace, happiness and honour. Those who have not lost their faith and pride in their own country will fight at our side. We will not expect to rest until these men are forced into submission.

This is the promise of the British Battalion to Britain.

INTERNATIONAL BRIGADE

National Memorial Meeting

PRO

Chairm

Barnet To

(Conductor: Arthu

Commentat

1. **Entrance of the British Battalions of the International Brigade**
2. **Roll Call**
3. **The Battalions Salute Spain**
4. **In Memoriam**

(During this part the audience is requested to stand)

Chopin's Funeral March

The Last Post

Silence

Poem: " To The Fallen "

(Recited by Selmar Vaz Dias)

Song: " Jarama Valley "

Sung by the men of the British Battalion and accompanied by the Clapham Accordion Band

Reveille

BRITISH BATTALION

Empress Hall, 7.30 p.m., Jan. 8th, 1939

AMME

Copeman
Prize Band
.G.S.M., A.T.C.L.)
e H. Bishop

5. **Mass Singing**
   Conducted by John Goss
   (For words of songs see overleaf)
6. **Harry Pollitt**
7. **Collection:** Ernest and Isabel Brown.
8. **Ellen Wilkinson, M.P.**
9. **Phillip Jordan**
10. **Negrin's Thirteen Points**
11. **Wilfrid Roberts, M.P.**
12. **Paul Robeson**
    (accompanied by Laurence Brown)
13. **Departure of the Battalion Convoy**

Music for Band and Trumpeters
and words of songs by Rufus Hogg.

Producer of Ceremonial — André Van Geyseghem.

Far from Their Homeland

Far from their homeland our comrades are lying
  Yet as they died 'twas with brothers they stood,
Fighting the cause of our common humanity,
  Healing its wounds with the gift of their blood.

  Chorus

Brave comrades we greet you,
  Ye are our leaders,
Yours is the faith that illumines our way;
  Pledged to the cause ye have sealed with your sacrifice
Naught can resist the people—Ours is the Day.

They who have fallen are building the future,
  We who remain are their head, hands and heart;
They saw a new world and strove for their vision,
  We swear to keep their trust and each play his part.

  Chorus

My Bonnie is over the Ocean

My Bonnie is over the ocean,
  My Bonnie is over the sea,
My Bonnie is over the ocean,
  O bring back my Bonnie to me.

Chorus:

Bring back, bring back,
  Bring back my Bonnie to me, to me;
Bring back, bring back,
  And bring back my Bonnie to me.

O blow, ye winds, over the ocean,
  And blow, ye winds, over the sea.
O blow, ye winds, over the ocean,
  And bring back my Bonnie to me.

Bring back, etc.

The wind has blown over the ocean,
  The wind has blown over the sea,
The wind has blown over the ocean,
  And brought back my Bonnie to me.

Brought back, etc.

We Shall Pass

(On sale in the hall.)

When Johnny Comes Marching Home

When Johnny comes marching home again,
  Hurrah! Hurrah!
We'll soon give the boot to What's his name,
  Hurrah! Hurrah!
We'll all unite with might and main
To lift the ban on Arms for Spain,
There'll be lots to do
When Johnny comes marching home!
There'll be lots to do
When Johnny comes marching home!

When Johnny comes marching home from Spain,
  Hurrah! Hurrah!
We'll see that he gets a job again,
  Hurrah! Hurrah!
And we pledge to those who died out there
To take their families in our care,
There'll be lots to do
When Johnny comes marching home!
There'll be lots to do
When Johnny comes marching home!

www.ingramcontent.com/pod-product-compliance
Lightning Source LLC
LaVergne TN
LVHW052355100826
845147LV00013B/849

9781474537933